Book 2: Old Watch Brands and Their Development

Horological Heritage From History to Investment : Exploring Brands, Collecting, and Investing

we embark on a captivating journey through time to explore the rich histories, remarkable achievements, and enduring legacies of some of the world's most esteemed watch brands. As we delve into the fascinating world of horology, we will uncover the stories behind these iconic brands, tracing their origins, milestones, and evolution over the years.

Watches have been an integral part of human history, not only serving as practical timekeeping instruments but also as symbols of style, craftsmanship, and heritage. Throughout the centuries, certain watch brands have established themselves as paragons of excellence, captivating the hearts of watch enthusiasts and collectors worldwide. From their pioneering innovations to their unwavering commitment to quality and precision, these old watch brands have shaped the very fabric of horology.

In this book, we will shine a spotlight on a diverse selection of old watch brands, each with its own distinctive identity and contribution to the watchmaking industry. We will delve into the remarkable stories behind brands that have stood the test of time, weathering challenges, and embracing the ever-changing landscape of watchmaking.

Our exploration will take us through the annals of history, unveiling the remarkable achievements of these watch brands and the visionary individuals who brought them to life. We will witness the birth of revolutionary watchmaking techniques, the introduction of groundbreaking complications, and the pursuit of artistic expression through intricate designs.

But this journey is not just a historical account; it is an invitation to discover the enduring allure of these old watch brands. We will uncover the secrets behind their enduring appeal, examining the factors that have propelled them to the pinnacle of the watch industry. From their commitment to impeccable craftsmanship to their relentless pursuit of innovation, we will unravel the qualities that have earned them a place of distinction in the hearts and minds of watch enthusiasts around the globe.

We will explore how these old watch brands have adapted and evolved over time, embracing new technologies, trends, and consumer preferences while staying true to their core values and traditions. We will witness the seamless fusion of tradition and modernity, as these brands continue to captivate the imagination of watch connoisseurs with their unwavering dedication to excellence.

Whether you are an avid watch collector, a history enthusiast, or simply someone intrigued by the artistry and heritage of watchmaking, this book will serve as a captivating guide. Join us as we embark on a journey through time, unlocking the captivating stories and timeless creations of old watch brands that have left an indelible mark on the world of horology.

So, without further ado, let us dive into the captivating world of old watch brands and their development, where the past comes alive, and the future unfolds with every tick of the hands.

Part 1: Overview of Old Watch Brands

Old watch brands carry with them a rich tapestry of history, innovation, and craftsmanship. They represent a tradition of excellence, embodying the spirit of ingenuity and artistry that has shaped the watchmaking industry over the centuries. By delving into their origins, philosophies, and signature characteristics, we will gain a deeper appreciation for the remarkable contributions they have made to horology.

In this part, we will unravel the allure and significance of old watch brands, examining the factors that have propelled them to the forefront of the industry. We will explore their founding stories, visionary leaders, and the core values that have guided their journey. From their humble beginnings to their current standing as esteemed horological icons, we will trace their evolution and highlight the milestones that have shaped their identity.

We will delve into the key distinguishing features that set these old watch brands apart. Each brand possesses a unique DNA that encapsulates its heritage, design language, and technical expertise. We will explore the iconic models, innovative complications, and distinctive design elements that have become synonymous with these brands, setting them apart from their competitors.

Our journey will also take us through the global impact of these old watch brands. We will examine their influence on the industry, their collaborations with other sectors, and their contributions to the wider world of luxury and craftsmanship. From the red carpet to the race track, these brands have left an indelible mark on popular culture and continue to captivate discerning individuals seeking the epitome of elegance and precision.

Whether you are a seasoned watch enthusiast, a collector seeking to expand your knowledge, or simply someone intrigued by the allure of old watch brands, this part of the book will provide you with a comprehensive understanding of their significance and enduring appeal. It will serve as a foundation for the deeper exploration that lies ahead, as we dive into the individual stories of these remarkable brands.

So, join us as we embark on this fascinating journey into the world of old watch brands. Through their histories, innovations, and legacies, we will discover the timeless beauty and exceptional craftsmanship that continue to captivate the hearts and minds of watch connoisseurs around the globe.

Introduction to vintage watch collecting and investment:

Exploring vintage watch collecting:

Vintage watch collecting has emerged as a captivating pursuit, captivating enthusiasts and investors alike. Beyond the mere function of telling time, vintage watches hold a distinct charm, offering a tangible connection to a bygone era. With their intricate craftsmanship, timeless designs, and historical significance, vintage watches have captivated the imagination of collectors worldwide. In this section, we will delve into the alluring world of vintage watch collecting, exploring its appeal, the growth it has experienced, and the exciting opportunities it presents as both a hobby and an investment avenue.

The Timeless Appeal of Vintage Watches:

Vintage watches possess an undeniable allure that stems from their authenticity, character, and enduring beauty. Each timepiece carries a unique story, reflecting the era in which it was created and the hands it has passed through over the years. Vintage watches capture the essence of craftsmanship and artistry, offering a glimpse into the evolution of watchmaking techniques and design sensibilities. The nostalgia and sentimental value associated with vintage watches add to their timeless appeal, making them cherished heirlooms and coveted collector's items.

The Growth of Vintage Watch Collecting:

In recent years, vintage watch collecting has witnessed a significant surge in popularity. The growing interest can be attributed to several factors. Firstly, vintage watches provide a distinctive alternative to the mass-produced timepieces of today, offering collectors a sense of individuality and exclusivity. Additionally, the rise of social media platforms and online communities has fostered a vibrant and interconnected vintage watch community, enabling enthusiasts to share their passion, knowledge, and discoveries. The accessibility of information and resources has fueled the growth of vintage watch collecting, attracting newcomers and seasoned collectors alike.

The Investment Potential of Vintage Watches:

Beyond the inherent beauty and sentimental value, vintage watches have also gained recognition as valuable investment assets. Collectors and investors have come to appreciate the potential for price appreciation in vintage watches, particularly those from renowned brands, limited editions, or with historical significance. Vintage watches, when acquired with careful consideration and thorough research, can offer attractive returns over time. However, it is important to note that investing in vintage watches requires expertise, market awareness, and a long-term perspective. The market for vintage watches is influenced by various factors, including brand reputation, rarity, condition, and current trends, which should be taken into account when building a vintage watch collection as an investment portfolio.

Navigating the Vintage Watch Market:

As with any collecting endeavor, navigating the vintage watch market requires knowledge, diligence, and discernment. It is essential to conduct thorough research, familiarize oneself with the specific brands, models, and historical context relevant to the desired collection. Understanding factors such as condition, authenticity, provenance, and market demand is crucial for making informed purchasing decisions. Engaging with reputable dealers, attending auctions, and seeking advice from experienced collectors can provide invaluable insights and guidance along the journey.

The Joy of Vintage Watch Collecting:

While the investment potential of vintage watches is undoubtedly intriguing, it is essential to remember that the true essence of vintage watch collecting lies in the joy and passion it brings. The process of acquiring, studying, and appreciating vintage timepieces is a fulfilling and enriching experience. Each vintage watch holds a story and carries with it a piece of history. The joy of discovering hidden gems, uncovering rare finds, and connecting with fellow collectors is what truly makes vintage watch collecting a remarkable pursuit.

Vintage watch collecting has captured the hearts of enthusiasts and investors worldwide, offering a gateway into the world of horological artistry, history, and craftsmanship. The appeal of vintage watches lies in their timeless beauty, distinctive character, and the unique stories they tell. Whether driven by passion, the desire to own a piece of history, or the potential for long-term value appreciation, vintage watch collecting presents an exciting journey of exploration and discovery. As we embark on this adventure, let us embrace the charm, elegance, and enduring allure of vintage watches, and celebrate the remarkable craftsmanship that has made them cherished artifacts of our collective heritage.

Historical significance:

Vintage watches offer more than just a glimpse into the past. They are tangible artifacts that encapsulate the craftsmanship, design principles, and cultural influences of the time in which they were created. Each vintage watch tells a unique story, representing a specific moment in horological history and reflecting the spirit of its era.

Craftsmanship:

Vintage watches stand as testaments to the meticulous craftsmanship and expertise of the watchmakers who brought them to life. In an age before advanced technology and automation, every component of a vintage watch was crafted and assembled by skilled hands. From the precision of the movements to the intricate details of the dial and case, vintage watches exemplify the artistry and dedication of the watchmakers of yesteryears.

Design:

Vintage watches exhibit an array of design styles that mirror the artistic movements and prevailing trends of their respective periods. From the elegant simplicity of Art Deco designs to the bold and vibrant aesthetics of the 1970s, each era left its imprint on watch design. Vintage watches capture the essence of their time, showcasing the creativity, innovation, and evolving tastes of the era in which they were created. The iconic designs of vintage watches continue to inspire modern watchmakers and serve as timeless references for contemporary timepiece creations.

Cultural context:

Vintage watches are not isolated from the broader cultural context of their time. They often mirror the social, economic, and political landscapes of their era. For example, the sleek and understated watches of the mid-20th century reflected the post-war era's focus on simplicity and functionality. On the other hand, the flamboyant and extravagant watches of the 1980s mirrored the exuberance and opulence of that era. Vintage watches provide a tangible connection to the history and culture of their time, allowing collectors to immerse themselves in the spirit of a bygone era.

By owning and appreciating vintage watches, collectors become custodians of horological heritage. These timepieces transcend their functionality and become conduits for understanding the craftsmanship, design principles, and cultural influences that shaped their creation. Vintage watches are not just mechanical marvels; they are living artifacts that bridge the gap between the past and the present, offering a window into the rich tapestry of human ingenuity and creativity.

As collectors explore the world of vintage watches, they embark on a journey of discovery, not only uncovering rare and unique timepieces but also gaining a deeper appreciation for the historical significance that these watches represent. Vintage watches allow us to connect with the past, to honor the master watchmakers who crafted them, and to celebrate the enduring legacy of horological artistry. In their presence, we are transported to different epochs, reliving the moments that have shaped our collective history.

In the world of vintage watch collecting, the historical significance of these timepieces adds another layer of depth and appreciation. By studying the craftsmanship, design, and cultural context of vintage watches, collectors gain a deeper understanding of the artistic and technological advancements that have shaped the evolution of timekeeping. Vintage watches serve as tangible links to our shared history, offering a tangible connection to the past and an opportunity to celebrate the artistry and ingenuity of the watchmakers who came before us.

Notable old watch brands and their historical significance:

Established luxury brands:

When it comes to the world of luxury watches, certain brands have established themselves as icons, synonymous with prestige, craftsmanship, and enduring quality. Rolex, Omega, Patek Philippe, and Audemars Piguet are among the esteemed watch brands that have shaped the watch industry and set the standards for excellence. Let's delve into the rich history and significant contributions of these established luxury brands:

Rolex:
Founded in 1905, Rolex is renowned for its innovation, precision, and timeless designs. The brand has introduced numerous pioneering technologies, such as the first waterproof wristwatch (the Rolex Oyster) and the first wristwatch with an automatically changing date (the Rolex Datejust). Rolex watches are known for their robustness, reliability, and association with exploration and achievement, as evidenced by their presence on the wrists of prominent figures like Sir Edmund Hillary and James Cameron.

Omega:
With a history dating back to 1848, Omega has a strong legacy of innovation and precision. The brand has been associated with significant milestones, including being the official timekeeper of the Olympic Games and the first watch worn on the moon during the Apollo missions. Omega watches are recognized for their sporty elegance, advanced mechanical movements, and enduring style. The Seamaster, Speedmaster, and Constellation are iconic collections that have stood the test of time.

Patek Philippe:
Founded in 1839, Patek Philippe is synonymous with refined elegance and exceptional craftsmanship. The brand is renowned for its complicated timepieces, including perpetual calendars, minute repeaters, and tourbillons. Patek Philippe watches are highly sought after by collectors for their artistry,

exclusivity, and investment value. Each timepiece is meticulously handcrafted, reflecting the brand's commitment to horological excellence and the pursuit of perfection.

Audemars Piguet:

Established in 1875, Audemars Piguet is known for its audacious designs, technical innovation, and masterful craftsmanship. The brand is particularly celebrated for its Royal Oak collection, designed by Gerald Genta in 1972, which revolutionized the luxury watch industry with its stainless steel case, octagonal bezel, and integrated bracelet. Audemars Piguet watches exemplify a blend of tradition and modernity, pushing the boundaries of watchmaking with complex movements and avant-garde aesthetics.

These established luxury brands have played a pivotal role in shaping the watch industry and setting the standards for craftsmanship, innovation, and desirability. Their contributions go beyond the creation of exquisite timepieces; they have defined the very essence of luxury and refined watchmaking. Each brand carries with it a rich heritage and a commitment to excellence, continuing to inspire and captivate watch enthusiasts and collectors around the world.

The influence of these brands extends beyond their individual timepieces. Their legacy and reputation have elevated the entire watch industry, establishing benchmarks for quality and design. As leaders in horology, Rolex, Omega, Patek Philippe, and Audemars Piguet have fostered a culture of excellence, driving innovation and inspiring other watchmakers to push the boundaries of what is possible.

For collectors and enthusiasts, owning a timepiece from one of these established luxury brands represents a connection to a storied history, a symbol of exceptional craftsmanship, and an investment in enduring value. These brands continue to shape the landscape of the watch industry, perpetuating their legacies and captivating generations of watch lovers with their unwavering commitment to horological artistry.

Regional or niche brands:

While established luxury brands like Rolex, Omega, Patek Philippe, and Audemars Piguet dominate the global watch market, there is a rich tapestry of regional or niche watch brands that have emerged with their own distinctive identities and loyal followings. These brands often showcase unique designs, exceptional craftsmanship, and a strong connection to their cultural or historical roots. Let's delve into the world of regional or niche watch brands that have garnered recognition:

Seiko (Japan):

Seiko, founded in 1881, is a Japanese watch brand that has become a global powerhouse. Known for its precise movements, innovation, and affordable luxury, Seiko offers a wide range of watches, from entry-level timepieces to high-end Grand Seiko models. Seiko's reputation for reliability and craftsmanship has earned it a dedicated fan base and a significant presence in the watch industry.

Nomos Glashütte (Germany):

Based in Glashütte, Germany, Nomos Glashütte is renowned for its minimalist designs and in-house movements. The brand focuses on clean aesthetics, exceptional accuracy, and accessible pricing. Nomos watches embody the Bauhaus design philosophy, combining simplicity with refined craftsmanship. The brand has received numerous accolades for its design and has successfully established itself as a prominent player in the luxury watch market.

Oris (Switzerland):

Oris, a Swiss watch brand founded in 1904, is known for its dedication to mechanical watchmaking and strong commitment to environmental causes. Oris offers a diverse range of watches, from rugged dive watches to elegant dress watches. The brand's Red Dot and Good Design award-winning timepieces showcase Swiss craftsmanship at more accessible price points, making them a popular choice for watch enthusiasts seeking quality and value.

Sinn (Germany):

Sinn, a German watch manufacturer, specializes in robust, functional timepieces with a focus on aviation and diving. The brand's watches are known for their durability, reliability, and innovative features such as antimagnetic cases, temperature resistance, and diving functionality. Sinn's dedication to creating purpose-driven watches has garnered a dedicated following among professionals and enthusiasts alike.

Baltic (France):

Baltic is a French watch brand that pays homage to vintage designs, particularly those from the mid-20th century. With their classic aesthetics and attention to detail, Baltic watches capture the nostalgia of the past while incorporating modern technology. The brand's limited-production models and meticulous craftsmanship have gained recognition among vintage watch enthusiasts and collectors.

Damasko (Germany):

Damasko is a German watch brand specializing in highly engineered and technologically advanced timepieces. The brand is known for its use of innovative materials, such as ice-hardened steel and Damasko's patented rotor systems. Damasko watches combine precision, durability, and distinctive design elements, making them popular choices among those seeking high-performance watches.

These regional or niche watch brands may not have the same global recognition as established luxury brands, but they have carved out a place in the watch industry through their unique designs, exceptional craftsmanship, and cultural or historical significance. They offer collectors and enthusiasts an opportunity to explore different styles, craftsmanship techniques, and narratives that reflect their specific regions or niche markets.

By embracing their regional or niche identities, these brands bring diversity and fresh perspectives to the watch market. They showcase the creativity, innovation, and craftsmanship that can be found beyond the traditional luxury watch brands, allowing collectors to discover hidden gems and create personal connections with timepieces that embody a particular cultural or historical context. Whether it's the precision of Seiko, the minimalist elegance of Nomos Glashütte, or the functional durability of Sinn, regional or niche brands offer a world of unique and captivating watches waiting to be explored.

Factors influencing the value of vintage watches:

Rarity and scarcity:

One of the factors that greatly influences the desirability and value of vintage watches is rarity and scarcity. The limited availability of certain models, whether due to low production numbers, discontinued production, or unique variations, creates a sense of exclusivity and adds to their allure among collectors. Here are some key points to consider regarding the impact of rarity and scarcity on vintage watch value:

Limited production numbers:
Vintage watches produced in limited quantities tend to be highly sought after by collectors. When a watch is produced in small numbers, it becomes rarer over time as the supply diminishes. Limited production can be intentional, such as when a brand releases special editions or commemorative models, or it can be a result of market demand and production constraints. The scarcity created by limited production numbers can drive up the value of these watches.

Discontinued models:
When a watch model is discontinued, it becomes increasingly difficult to find in the market. Collectors often seek out these discontinued models, as they become more scarce over time. The discontinuation of a watch can be due to various reasons, including changes in brand strategy, technological advancements, or evolving consumer preferences. Discontinued models can hold significant value as they represent a specific era or design aesthetic that is no longer in production.

Unique variations:
Some vintage watches possess unique variations that make them even more desirable to collectors. These variations can include special dials, different case materials, specific dial configurations, or rare features. These unique characteristics set them apart from the standard models and make them highly

sought after. Collectors appreciate the individuality and rarity of these variations, which can significantly impact their value.

Historical significance:

Vintage watches with historical significance or associations can also contribute to their rarity and collectibility. Watches that were owned or worn by notable individuals, connected to important events, or linked to significant milestones in the watch industry tend to command higher values. The historical context and provenance of a watch add an extra layer of appeal for collectors who appreciate the stories and narratives associated with these timepieces.

Market demand and collector preferences:

The rarity and scarcity of vintage watches are ultimately driven by market demand and collector preferences. The desirability of certain brands, models, or specific variations can fluctuate over time, influenced by factors such as changing trends, cultural influences, and the overall interest in vintage watch collecting. It's important to stay informed about market dynamics and understand the preferences of collectors to gauge the potential value and collectibility of vintage watches.

In the world of vintage watches, rarity and scarcity play a significant role in establishing the value and collectibility of timepieces. Limited production numbers, discontinued models, and unique variations all contribute to the exclusivity and desirability among collectors. It is the combination of craftsmanship, historical significance, and rarity that makes these vintage watches highly sought after and cherished by enthusiasts worldwide.

Historical context and provenance:

The historical context and provenance of a vintage watch can greatly enhance its desirability and market value. When a watch is connected to significant historical events, famous owners, or notable stories, it adds an extra layer of intrigue and collectibility. Here are some key points to consider regarding the impact of historical context and provenance on vintage watch value:

Historical events:

Vintage watches that were present during important historical events often carry a unique appeal. For example, watches worn by military personnel during wars, expeditions, or significant cultural moments hold a special place in collectors' hearts. The association with historical events adds a sense of authenticity and can evoke a nostalgic connection to the past. Watches that have witnessed or played a role in shaping history are highly prized by collectors who appreciate the stories they carry.

Famous owners:

Vintage watches that were owned or worn by famous individuals, such as celebrities, politicians, athletes, or cultural icons, can command significant attention and value. The association with a notable owner adds glamour, prestige, and a sense of provenance to the watch. Collectors are often fascinated by the idea of owning a timepiece that was once part of the personal collection of someone admired or revered. The ownership history of a vintage watch can elevate its status and make it highly sought after in the market.

Notable stories and anecdotes:

Vintage watches with interesting stories or unique anecdotes attached to them capture the imagination of collectors. These stories can range from tales of remarkable craftsmanship, extraordinary feats of engineering, or even tales of adventure and discovery. Whether it's a watch that survived extreme conditions, accompanied a daring expedition, or has an unusual origin, these stories create a sense of mystique and intrigue. The narrative surrounding a vintage watch can enhance its desirability and market value.

Provenance and documentation:

The availability of comprehensive documentation and provenance supporting a vintage watch's history can significantly impact its value. Authenticity and a clear, traceable ownership history provide confidence to collectors and investors. Documentation can include original papers, service records, receipts, and even photographs of the watch in its historical context. The more complete and well-documented the provenance, the higher the level of trust and value attributed to the watch.

Cultural and artistic significance:

Vintage watches that embody the cultural and artistic movements of their respective eras hold a special place in the hearts of collectors. Whether it's a watch that represents the Art Deco period, the sleek minimalism of the mid-20th century, or the avant-garde designs of the 1970s, these watches are appreciated for their artistic and cultural contributions. The influence of design movements, craftsmanship techniques, and cultural trends can elevate the desirability and value of vintage watches.

When considering vintage watches, the historical context and provenance add depth and richness to the timepieces. Historical events, famous owners, notable stories, and cultural significance all contribute to the desirability and market value of these watches. Collectors are drawn to the stories behind the watches, connecting them to a broader narrative and appreciating their place in history. The combination of exceptional craftsmanship and captivating stories makes vintage watches with a compelling historical context and provenance highly sought after in the world of collecting.

Design and aesthetics:

The design and aesthetics of vintage watches play a significant role in their desirability and value. Certain watches have become iconic for their groundbreaking designs, innovative features, or artistic elements that set them apart from others. Here are some key factors to consider regarding the influence of design and aesthetics on the value of vintage watches:

Iconic designs:

Some vintage watches have achieved legendary status due to their iconic designs. These designs often become synonymous with the brand and era they represent. Examples include the Rolex Submariner, Omega Speedmaster, and Patek Philippe Nautilus. These watches feature distinctive shapes, dial layouts, and overall aesthetics that have stood the test of time. The enduring popularity and recognition of these designs contribute to their value and collectibility.

Innovative features:

Vintage watches that introduced innovative features or technological advancements during their time are highly sought after by collectors. These features can range from groundbreaking movements, complications, or materials. For instance, the introduction of the first automatic chronograph movement, the Zenith El Primero, revolutionized the watch industry. Vintage watches with innovative features that were ahead of their time hold a special place in collectors' hearts and can command premium prices.

Artistic elements:

Vintage watches often exhibit exquisite artistic elements that enhance their value. These elements can include intricate dial designs, enamel work, guilloché patterns, or hand-engraved cases. Artistic craftsmanship adds a touch of elegance, uniqueness, and refinement to a watch. Vintage watches with exceptional artistic elements are highly prized by collectors who appreciate the fusion of horological and artistic mastery.

Influential designers:

The involvement of renowned designers or collaborations with notable artists can elevate the desirability and value of vintage watches. The contribution of influential designers such as Gerald Genta, who created iconic designs for Audemars Piguet Royal Oak and Patek Philippe Nautilus, or collaborations with artists like Salvador Dalí or Andy Warhol, adds a layer of artistic prestige and collector appeal. Vintage watches associated with celebrated designers or artists are considered highly collectible and can command premium prices.

Period-specific aesthetics:

Vintage watches often reflect the design aesthetics of their respective eras, capturing the essence of a particular time period. Watches from the Art Deco era, for example, feature geometric shapes and intricate detailing, while watches from the 1960s embrace bold colors and futuristic designs. These period-specific aesthetics evoke a sense of nostalgia and are valued by collectors who appreciate the artistic expression of a particular era.

Rarity and uniqueness:

Vintage watches that feature rare or unique design elements are highly sought after by collectors. Limited production models, discontinued variations, or prototype designs often carry a sense of exclusivity and scarcity. Collectors are drawn to these watches as they offer a chance to own something truly distinctive and exceptional.

The design and aesthetics of vintage watches contribute significantly to their desirability, collectibility, and value. Iconic designs, innovative features, artistic elements, influential designers, period-specific aesthetics, and rarity all play a role in elevating the value of vintage watches. Collectors are captivated by the beauty, craftsmanship, and innovation displayed in these watches, and they appreciate the timeless appeal and artistic expression that vintage timepieces embody.

Market trends and collecting strategies for old watch brands:

Collector preferences and trends:

The world of vintage watch collecting is dynamic, with collector preferences and trends continuously evolving. Understanding the shifting tastes and preferences of collectors is essential for those interested in building a vintage watch collection. Here are some key factors to consider regarding collector preferences and trends in the vintage watch market:

Brand popularity:

Certain brands have consistently enjoyed a strong following among vintage watch collectors. Brands such as Rolex, Omega, Patek Philippe, and Audemars Piguet have established themselves as pillars of the vintage watch market, with a rich history, exceptional craftsmanship, and iconic models. These brands continue to be highly sought after due to their reputation for quality, timeless designs, and enduring value.

Model desirability:

Within popular brands, specific models often capture collectors' attention and become highly coveted. These models may possess unique features, historical significance, or a combination of factors that make them particularly desirable. Examples include the Rolex Daytona, Omega Seamaster 300, Patek Philippe Calatrava, and Audemars Piguet Royal Oak. Collectors closely follow trends and pay close attention to the desirability and market demand of specific models.

Design eras:

Vintage watch collectors often develop preferences for particular design eras based on aesthetic appeal and historical significance. Design eras such as Art Deco, Mid-Century Modern, or the 1970s "Me Decade" have distinctive design elements and characteristics that resonate with collectors. Preferences can shift over time as collectors explore different eras and discover new design influences.

Retro and nostalgia:

The current trend of embracing retro styles and nostalgia has also influenced the vintage watch market. Collectors are drawn to watches that evoke a sense of nostalgia and embody the spirit of a bygone era. Vintage watches from the 1960s and 1970s, with their bold colors, unique shapes, and futuristic designs, have experienced increased popularity due to their retro appeal.

Independent watchmakers:

In recent years, there has been a growing interest in independent watchmakers and their unique creations. These watchmakers often produce limited-edition or bespoke watches with a strong emphasis on craftsmanship and artistic expression. Collectors seeking something different and exclusive are attracted to the creativity and innovation offered by independent watchmakers.

Social media and online communities:

The advent of social media platforms and online communities dedicated to vintage watches has played a significant role in shaping collector preferences and trends. These platforms provide a space for enthusiasts to share their collections, discuss watches, and showcase rare finds. They also facilitate the spread of information about specific models, brands, and design trends, influencing collector preferences and creating a sense of community.

Sustainable and ethical considerations:

In recent years, there has been a growing awareness and emphasis on sustainable and ethical practices in the watch industry. Vintage watches, with their inherent durability and longevity, are seen as a sustainable choice compared to buying new watches. Collectors may prioritize vintage watches as a way to support sustainability initiatives and reduce environmental impact.

Investment potential:

While many collectors are driven by a passion for vintage watches, the potential for investment and value appreciation is also a consideration. Certain watches or brands may gain attention and increase in value over time, making them attractive from an investment standpoint. Collectors closely monitor market trends, auction results, and expert opinions to identify watches with potential for future value growth.

It is important to note that collector preferences and trends can vary regionally and across different segments of the vintage watch market. Keeping abreast of industry news, engaging with the watch collecting community, and conducting thorough research are key to understanding and staying informed about current collector preferences and emerging trends. Ultimately, building a vintage watch collection that aligns with individual tastes and passions while also considering collector preferences and market trends can lead to a rewarding and fulfilling collecting experience.

Collecting strategies:

When it comes to vintage watch collecting, there are various strategies that collectors can adopt based on their personal preferences, goals, and budget. Here are some popular collecting strategies to consider:

Brand-focused collecting:

Some collectors choose to focus their collection on specific watch brands. This strategy allows them to delve deep into the history, craftsmanship, and distinct characteristics of a particular brand. By acquiring a range of models from a specific brand, collectors can create a comprehensive collection that showcases the brand's evolution over time. The benefit of brand-focused collecting is the opportunity to become an expert in that brand, understanding its nuances, and appreciating its unique offerings.

Model-specific collecting:

This strategy involves collecting different variations or iterations of a particular watch model. Collectors may choose to specialize in a specific model that holds historical significance, iconic status, or features innovative design elements. By acquiring different versions or limited editions of the same model, collectors can explore the evolution and subtle variations of a beloved timepiece. Model-specific collecting allows for a focused and in-depth understanding of a single watch model's history, popularity, and market value.

Theme-based collecting:

Some collectors opt for a thematic approach, focusing on watches that share a common theme, such as military watches, dive watches, chronographs, or complications. This strategy allows collectors to explore a specific category of watches in depth, appreciating the unique features and historical context associated with the chosen theme. Theme-based collecting offers the opportunity to curate a cohesive and specialized collection that tells a story or reflects a particular interest.

Historical period collecting:

Collecting vintage watches from a specific historical period is another popular approach. This strategy allows collectors to immerse themselves in a particular era and appreciate the designs, craftsmanship, and cultural influences of that time. For example, collecting watches from the Art Deco period of the 1920s and 1930s showcases the elegant and geometric designs of that era, while collecting watches from the 1970s emphasizes bold colors and avant-garde styles. Historical period collecting offers a chance to capture the spirit and aesthetics of a specific time in horological history.

Rarity-driven collecting:

Some collectors prioritize acquiring rare and highly sought-after watches. This approach involves focusing on limited-edition models, discontinued watches, or those with unique variations or complications. Collectors who appreciate the thrill of the hunt and the exclusivity of owning rare timepieces find this strategy particularly appealing. Rarity-driven collecting often requires diligence and extensive research to identify and acquire these elusive watches, but the potential reward is the satisfaction of owning truly exceptional and valuable pieces.

Each collecting strategy has its own benefits and challenges. Focusing on specific brands or models allows for a deep understanding and expertise in a particular area. Theme-based collecting offers the opportunity to explore a specific category or interest. Historical period collecting allows collectors to immerse themselves in a specific era's design and cultural context. Rarity-driven collecting offers the excitement of owning unique and sought-after timepieces.

It's important for collectors to align their collecting strategy with their personal interests, budget, and long-term goals. Whether one chooses to adopt a single strategy or combine multiple approaches, the key is to enjoy the journey of collecting, continually educate oneself, and engage with the passionate community of vintage watch enthusiasts. By carefully selecting a collecting strategy, collectors can build a collection that reflects their individual tastes, tells a story, and brings them joy and satisfaction.

Preservation and restoration:

One of the unique aspects of collecting vintage watches is the challenge of striking a balance between preserving the originality and patina of a timepiece and ensuring its proper maintenance and functionality. Here, we delve into the importance of preservation, the potential need for restoration, and how these factors impact the value of vintage watches.

Preservation:

Preserving the originality and patina of a vintage watch is often highly valued among collectors. The original dial, hands, case, and other components that have aged naturally over time can contribute to the watch's charm, character, and historical authenticity. Collectors appreciate the unique story that the patina and wear of a vintage watch tell, reflecting its journey through time. Preservation efforts involve handling the watch with care, protecting it from excessive exposure to sunlight, moisture, and extreme temperatures, and avoiding unnecessary polishing or refinishing. Collectors often seek watches in their original condition, with intact components, including original dials, hands, and crowns, as these factors contribute to the watch's originality and value.

Restoration:

While preservation is highly regarded, there are instances where restoration becomes necessary to maintain the value and functionality of a vintage watch. Restoration involves carefully repairing or replacing worn or damaged components to bring the watch back to its original condition. This can include refinishing the case, reluming the hands, or replacing worn-out parts such as crystals, gaskets, or movements.
Restoration requires a skilled and experienced watchmaker who understands the intricacies of vintage timepieces. It is important to note that restoration should be approached with caution to ensure that the watch retains its historical integrity and doesn't lose its originality. Over-restoration or improper techniques can diminish the value of a vintage watch and compromise its authenticity.

Balancing preservation and restoration:

The balance between preservation and restoration is a delicate one. Collectors and enthusiasts must carefully consider the condition of a vintage watch and its impact on both its aesthetic appeal and value. Watches in pristine, original condition are often highly sought after and command higher prices due to their rarity. However, if a watch requires certain repairs or restoration to ensure proper functioning, it may be necessary to strike a balance between preserving its originality and ensuring its reliability.

Transparency in the restoration process is crucial. Documenting any restoration work undertaken, such as noting replaced parts or refinishing, is important for future buyers and collectors. This information provides clarity about the watch's history and can help preserve its value over time.

The decision to preserve or restore a vintage watch depends on the specific watch, its condition, and the collector's preferences. While preserving originality and patina is often favored, it is essential to address necessary maintenance and repairs to keep the watch in good working order. Seeking the advice of reputable watchmakers, restorers, and experts in the vintage watch community can provide valuable guidance in making informed decisions about preservation and restoration.

The balance between preservation and restoration is an integral part of the vintage watch collecting journey. It involves carefully considering the condition of a watch, understanding the impact of preservation and restoration on its value, and making informed decisions to maintain the watch's authenticity and functionality. By striking the right balance, collectors can ensure that their vintage watches retain their historical significance, allure, and long-term value.

.

Part 2: Exploring Vintage Watch Brands

From iconic names that have shaped the watchmaking industry to hidden gems that have gained recognition among collectors, this section delves into the stories, innovations, and enduring legacies of these renowned timepiece manufacturers.

Vintage watch brands hold a special place in the hearts of enthusiasts and collectors. They not only encapsulate the artistry and craftsmanship of a bygone era but also represent the evolution of horology and the milestones achieved throughout history. In this section, we uncover the rich heritage and distinctive characteristics of vintage watch brands, allowing you to delve into their captivating narratives and appreciate the artistry that has made them enduring icons.

We begin our exploration with the established luxury brands, whose names have become synonymous with prestige and excellence. Brands such as Rolex, Omega, Patek Philippe, and Audemars Piguet have left an indelible mark on the watchmaking landscape. We delve into their illustrious histories, remarkable innovations, and the enduring appeal that has made them the benchmarks of luxury and refinement.

But our journey doesn't stop there. We also shine a spotlight on regional or niche brands that have carved their own unique paths in the world of watchmaking. These brands may be lesser-known on a global scale but have gained recognition for their exceptional designs, craftsmanship, and historical significance. We explore the stories behind these brands and how they have contributed to the diversity and vibrancy of the watch industry.

Rarity and scarcity are essential elements that contribute to the allure of vintage watches. Limited production numbers, discontinued models, and unique variations can elevate the value and collectibility of these timepieces. We delve into the world of rarity and scarcity, unraveling the factors that make certain vintage watches highly coveted among collectors.

Beyond the rarity, we explore the significance of historical context and provenance. Historical events, famous owners, and notable stories associated with specific vintage watches can captivate the imagination and add layers of desirability and value. We unravel the tales behind these timepieces, showcasing how their historical context and provenance make them cherished artifacts in the eyes of collectors.

Design and aesthetics have always been integral to the appeal of vintage watches. We celebrate the iconic designs, innovative features, and artistic elements that have made certain vintage watches timeless masterpieces. Whether it's the elegance of a dress watch, the sporty allure of a chronograph, or the avant-garde aesthetics of a unique design, we explore the design influences and artistic elements that continue to captivate collectors worldwide.

We examine the ever-evolving tastes and preferences of vintage watch collectors. Trends come and go, and the market fluctuates, but the passion for vintage watches remains. We dive into collector preferences and the factors that influence their choices, from the popularity of specific brands and models to the design eras that capture their imagination. Understanding collector preferences and trends allows you to navigate the vintage watch market with insight and make informed decisions about your own collection.

Historical background and significance of each vintage watch brand:

Rolex:

Rolex, a name that resonates with luxury, precision, and timeless elegance, has cemented its position as one of the most esteemed and sought-after brands in the vintage watch market. With a history spanning over a century, Rolex has consistently pushed the boundaries of horological innovation and craftsmanship, leaving an indelible mark on the watchmaking industry.

Our exploration of vintage watch brands wouldn't be complete without delving into the captivating story of Rolex. Founded in 1905 by Hans Wilsdorf and Alfred Davis in London, Rolex began its journey with a vision to create wristwatches that were not only accurate and reliable but also elegant and durable. This vision laid the foundation for the brand's enduring success.

Throughout its history, Rolex has introduced numerous groundbreaking innovations that have revolutionized the watchmaking industry. One of the notable milestones in Rolex's legacy is the introduction of the Oyster case in 1926. This groundbreaking invention, characterized by its hermetically sealed case, made Rolex the pioneer of waterproof watches. The Oyster case, combined with the self-winding Perpetual movement introduced in 1931, set a new standard for durability and precision in watchmaking.

Rolex's commitment to precision timekeeping led to the brand's achievement of the prestigious Swiss Official Chronometer Certification in 1910, making it one of the first watchmakers to receive this distinction. The brand's dedication to accuracy is further exemplified by its introduction of the COSC (Contrôle Officiel Suisse des Chronomètres) certification, ensuring that each Rolex timepiece meets the highest standards of precision.

Iconic models have played a pivotal role in Rolex's enduring popularity and desirability among collectors. One of the most iconic models in the brand's lineup is the Rolex Submariner, introduced in 1953 as the world's first dive watch. With its robust construction, rotating bezel, and distinctive design, the Submariner quickly became a symbol of adventure and exploration. Other iconic models, such as the Rolex Daytona, GMT-Master, and Datejust, have also etched themselves into the horological pantheon, capturing the imaginations of watch enthusiasts worldwide.

Rolex's commitment to excellence extends to its in-house manufacturing capabilities. The brand is known for its vertically integrated production process, where every component of a Rolex watch is meticulously crafted and assembled in-house. This level of control allows Rolex to maintain exceptional quality and ensure the longevity of its timepieces.

In the vintage watch market, Rolex's reputation for precision, durability, and timeless design has propelled it to great heights. The scarcity of certain vintage Rolex models, combined with their historical significance and enduring appeal, has made them highly coveted among collectors. From the classic elegance of the Datejust to the rugged sportiness of the Explorer, each vintage Rolex timepiece carries with it a legacy of fine craftsmanship and horological excellence.

Omega:

When it comes to vintage watches, few brands carry the same level of prestige and historical significance as Omega. For over a century, Omega has been at the forefront of horological innovation, capturing the hearts of collectors with its exceptional craftsmanship, pioneering spirit, and enduring style.

Omega's journey began in 1848, when Louis Brandt founded a small workshop in La Chaux-de-Fonds, Switzerland. From its humble beginnings, Omega quickly gained recognition for its precision and reliability. The brand's commitment to accuracy led to numerous awards and world records, establishing Omega as a symbol of excellence in timekeeping.

One of Omega's most significant contributions to watchmaking came in 1894 with the introduction of the Omega caliber. This breakthrough movement, known for its innovative features and exceptional precision, laid the foundation for the brand's future success. The Omega caliber became the benchmark for accuracy, setting the stage for Omega's remarkable achievements in the years to come.

Omega's legacy in the realm of space exploration is legendary. In 1962, the Omega Speedmaster made history as it became the first watch to be worn on the moon during the Apollo 11 mission. This iconic moment solidified Omega's place in horological history and sparked a fascination with space-themed watches that endures to this day. The Speedmaster's association with NASA and its status as the "Moonwatch" have made it one of the most sought-after vintage models among collectors.

Beyond its connection to space exploration, Omega has produced a range of notable vintage models that have captured the attention of watch enthusiasts. The Omega Seamaster, with its elegant yet robust design, has become synonymous with diving watches, particularly due to its association with the British Royal Navy and James Bond films. The Omega Constellation, with its iconic "Griffes" or claws, represents the brand's dedication to precision and refinement. Other notable vintage models, such as the Omega Railmaster and Omega De Ville, have also left an indelible mark on the world of horology.

Omega's commitment to innovation extends beyond its movements. The brand has continuously pushed boundaries in terms of design, materials, and technological advancements. From the use of ceramic bezels and Liquidmetal alloys to the incorporation of Co-Axial escapements, Omega has consistently embraced innovation to enhance the performance and durability of its timepieces.

In the world of vintage watches, Omega's rich heritage and association with exploration, precision, and style have elevated it to the status of a true horological icon. Collectors are drawn to the unique combination of historical significance, exceptional craftsmanship, and timeless design that defines Omega's vintage models.

Patek Philippe:

When it comes to luxury timepieces, few names command as much reverence and admiration as Patek Philippe. With a history dating back to 1839, Patek Philippe has established itself as a pinnacle of watchmaking excellence, renowned for its exceptional craftsmanship, timeless designs, and uncompromising commitment to quality.

Patek Philippe's reputation as one of the most prestigious watch brands in the world is rooted in its unwavering pursuit of perfection. Each Patek Philippe watch is a testament to the brand's unwavering dedication to precision and artistry. From the meticulous hand-finishing of every component to the intricate complications that adorn its timepieces, Patek Philippe exemplifies the pinnacle of Swiss watchmaking tradition.

At the heart of Patek Philippe's success lies its commitment to artisanal craftsmanship. The brand's skilled watchmakers, engravers, and enamellers work tirelessly to create timepieces of exceptional beauty and technical complexity. Patek Philippe has been instrumental in preserving and advancing the art of handcraftsmanship, showcasing exquisite enamel dials, delicate guilloché patterns, and intricate hand-engraved motifs that elevate its watches to wearable works of art.

Patek Philippe is renowned for its extraordinary complications, which are masterfully integrated into its timepieces. From perpetual calendars and chronographs to minute repeaters and tourbillons, Patek Philippe pushes the boundaries of mechanical watchmaking with its innovative and meticulously executed complications. These complex mechanisms not only serve practical functions but also exemplify the brand's commitment to technical innovation and excellence.

The enduring appeal of Patek Philippe lies not only in its technical mastery but also in its timeless designs. Patek Philippe watches exhibit an understated elegance and classic aesthetics that transcend fleeting trends. The brand's iconic models, such as the Calatrava, Nautilus, and Aquanaut, have become symbols of refined luxury, coveted by collectors and watch enthusiasts around the world.

Patek Philippe's commitment to exclusivity and rarity further contributes to its desirability. The brand produces a limited number of watches each year, ensuring that each timepiece remains an object of rarity and exclusivity. Patek Philippe's strict control over its production and distribution channels ensures that its watches retain their value and desirability over time.

Owning a Patek Philippe watch is a statement of refined taste, appreciation for exceptional craftsmanship, and an understanding of horological artistry. Patek Philippe timepieces are not simply watches; they are heirlooms that can be passed down through generations, carrying with them a legacy of excellence and enduring value.

Audemars Piguet:

When it comes to the world of luxury watchmaking, few brands have made as profound an impact as Audemars Piguet. Established in 1875 in the picturesque Vallée de Joux in Switzerland, Audemars Piguet has become synonymous with exquisite craftsmanship, cutting-edge design, and uncompromising innovation.

At the core of Audemars Piguet's success lies its unwavering commitment to pushing the boundaries of watchmaking. The brand has a long history of introducing groundbreaking timepieces that challenge traditional conventions and redefine what is possible in terms of design and engineering. From pioneering the use of unconventional materials to introducing revolutionary complications, Audemars Piguet has consistently pushed the limits of horological innovation.

One of Audemars Piguet's most iconic creations is the Royal Oak collection, which revolutionized the industry when it was introduced in 1972. Designed by the legendary watch designer Gérald Genta, the Royal Oak was the world's first luxury sports watch crafted in stainless steel. Its bold and distinctive octagonal shape, integrated bracelet, and exposed screws defied the norms of traditional luxury watch design and established a new aesthetic paradigm.

The Royal Oak's impact on the industry cannot be overstated. It not only redefined the concept of luxury sports watches but also set the stage for the trend of high-end steel timepieces that continues to dominate the market today. The Royal Oak's success paved the way for subsequent iconic models within the collection, including the Royal Oak Offshore and Royal Oak Concept, each pushing the boundaries of design and functionality.

Beyond the Royal Oak, Audemars Piguet has continued to create exceptional timepieces characterized by impeccable craftsmanship and innovative complications. The brand's commitment to in-house manufacturing and hand-finishing of its movements ensures that each Audemars Piguet watch meets the highest standards of quality and precision. From intricate tourbillons and perpetual calendars to striking minute repeaters, Audemars Piguet showcases its technical mastery and horological expertise.

Audemars Piguet's dedication to exclusivity and limited production further enhances the desirability of its watches. By maintaining a relatively low production volume, the brand ensures that each timepiece remains a coveted rarity. This exclusivity, coupled with the brand's commitment to impeccable craftsmanship and innovative design, has attracted a discerning clientele of watch collectors and enthusiasts.

Owning an Audemars Piguet watch signifies an appreciation for horological excellence, cutting-edge design, and a bold approach to watchmaking. Each Audemars Piguet timepiece is a testament to the brand's rich heritage and relentless pursuit of perfection. Whether it's the iconic Royal Oak collection or the exceptional complications found in other Audemars Piguet models, owning a piece from this esteemed brand is an expression of individuality and a connection to a legacy of innovation.

Evolution and development of vintage watch brands:

Brand milestones:

Every vintage watch brand has a unique journey marked by significant milestones, innovations, and design changes that have defined their identity and contributed to their enduring success. These milestones not only showcase the evolution of the brand but also reflect the broader developments in the watch industry. Let's delve into the key brand milestones of Rolex, Omega, Patek Philippe, and Audemars Piguet.

Rolex:

Rolex has left an indelible mark on the watch industry with its commitment to precision, durability, and timeless design. Over its illustrious history, Rolex has achieved several notable milestones that have solidified its position as one of the world's most renowned watch brands. Some of the key milestones include:

Invention of the Oyster Case: In 1926, Rolex introduced the Oyster case, the world's first waterproof watch case. This groundbreaking innovation revolutionized watchmaking by ensuring that watches could withstand water and dust, making them reliable and durable timepieces.

Introduction of the Perpetual Movement: In 1931, Rolex unveiled the Perpetual movement, the first self-winding mechanism with a perpetual rotor. This automatic winding system eliminated the need for manual winding and set the standard for modern self-winding watches.

Achievement of Chronometer Certification: Rolex's commitment to precision led to its achievement of chronometer certification for its watches. In 1910, Rolex became the first watchmaker to receive the Swiss Certificate of Chronometric Precision, a testament to the brand's accuracy and reliability.

Omega:

Omega has a rich history of innovation, technical excellence, and remarkable achievements that have cemented its status as a leading watch brand. Here are some of the key milestones in Omega's journey:

Olympic Timing: Omega's association with the Olympic Games dates back to 1932 when the brand became the official timekeeper for the event. Since then, Omega has played a pivotal role in timing the world's most prestigious sporting event, setting new standards in precision and accuracy.

Speedmaster and Space Exploration: In 1965, NASA selected the Omega Speedmaster as the official watch for its astronauts. This historic moment led to the Speedmaster's iconic status as the first watch worn on the moon during the Apollo 11 mission in 1969, solidifying its place in space exploration history.

Co-Axial Escapement: Omega introduced the Co-Axial escapement in 1999, a significant breakthrough in watchmaking. This innovative mechanism reduces friction in the movement, improving accuracy and long-term performance while requiring less frequent servicing.

Patek Philippe:

Patek Philippe is renowned for its exquisite craftsmanship, exceptional complications, and timelessly elegant designs. The brand's milestones exemplify its dedication to horological excellence. Here are some noteworthy milestones in Patek Philippe's legacy:

Invention of the Perpetual Calendar: Patek Philippe introduced the first wristwatch with a perpetual calendar in 1925. This complication automatically accounts for the varying lengths of months and leap years, displaying the correct date without requiring manual adjustment.

Introduction of the Nautilus: In 1976, Patek Philippe launched the Nautilus, a sports luxury watch designed by Gérald Genta. Its distinctive porthole-inspired design and robust construction challenged the prevailing notion that sports watches had to be purely functional, establishing a new trend for luxury sports timepieces.

Patek Philippe Museum: In 2001, Patek Philippe opened its own museum in Geneva, Switzerland. The museum houses an extensive collection of historical timepieces, showcasing the brand's rich heritage and its significant contributions to watchmaking.

Audemars Piguet:

Audemars Piguet has carved a unique path in the watch industry through its innovative spirit and commitment to exceptional craftsmanship. The brand's milestones reflect its relentless pursuit of horological excellence:

Introduction of the Royal Oak: In 1972, Audemars Piguet launched the iconic Royal Oak, a luxury sports watch crafted in stainless steel. Designed by Gérald Genta, the Royal Oak defied conventional design norms and established a new genre of high-end sports watches.

Development of Complications: Audemars Piguet is renowned for its expertise in crafting intricate and sophisticated complications. The brand has introduced numerous groundbreaking complications, including the first self-winding tourbillon wristwatch in 1986 and the Royal Oak Concept with its avant-garde designs and innovative features.

Le Brassus Manufacture: Audemars Piguet's Le Brassus Manufacture, located in the Vallée de Joux, Switzerland, serves as the brand's headquarters and production facility. The manufacture combines traditional watchmaking techniques with modern technology, ensuring the highest level of craftsmanship and quality.

These brand milestones are a testament to the enduring legacy of Rolex, Omega, Patek Philippe, and Audemars Piguet. Each brand's achievements have contributed to the advancement of watchmaking, showcasing their unwavering commitment to innovation, precision, and timeless design. As we delve further into the vintage watch brands in this book, we will explore their unique stories, notable achievements, and the exceptional timepieces that have captivated collectors and enthusiasts worldwide.

Influential models:

Within the vast repertoire of vintage watches, certain models stand out as pivotal in the development and market presence of renowned watch brands.

These influential models not only embody the brand's vision and expertise but also hold a special place in the hearts of collectors and enthusiasts. Let's explore some of these iconic vintage watch models that have shaped the legacy of Rolex, Omega, Patek Philippe, and Audemars Piguet.

Rolex:

Rolex Submariner: Introduced in 1953, the Rolex Submariner became the archetype of the modern diving watch. Its robust construction, water resistance, and iconic design have made it an enduring symbol of adventure and exploration.

Rolex Daytona: Originally designed for professional race car drivers, the Rolex Daytona has become synonymous with high-performance chronographs. Its distinctive dial, tachymeter bezel, and precision movement have solidified its status as an iconic sports watch.

Omega:

Omega Speedmaster Professional: The Omega Speedmaster Professional, also known as the "Moonwatch," achieved legendary status as the first watch worn on the moon during the Apollo 11 mission in 1969. Its durability, chronograph functionality, and association with space exploration have made it an iconic timepiece.

Omega Seamaster 300: The Omega Seamaster 300, introduced in 1957, was designed as a professional diver's watch. Its robust construction, water resistance, and classic design have made it a highly sought-after vintage model.

Patek Philippe:

Patek Philippe Calatrava: The Calatrava exemplifies Patek Philippe's commitment to timeless elegance and understated luxury. Its clean, minimalist design and exquisite craftsmanship have made it a classic dress watch and an enduring symbol of sophistication.

Patek Philippe Nautilus: The Nautilus, designed by Gérald Genta, revolutionized the luxury sports watch genre with its distinctive porthole-inspired design. Its combination of refined aesthetics and robust construction has contributed to its iconic status.

Audemars Piguet:

Audemars Piguet Royal Oak: The Royal Oak, introduced in 1972, challenged traditional watch design with its octagonal shape, integrated bracelet, and exposed screws. Its bold and audacious design redefined the concept of luxury sports watches.

Audemars Piguet Royal Oak Offshore: Building upon the success of the Royal Oak, the Royal Oak Offshore pushed the boundaries of sports watch design even further. With its larger case size, rugged construction, and daring aesthetics, it has become a symbol of contemporary luxury.

These influential models from Rolex, Omega, Patek Philippe, and Audemars Piguet have not only left an indelible mark on the vintage watch market but also continue to inspire and captivate collectors with their timeless appeal and exceptional craftsmanship. As we delve deeper into the world of vintage watches, we will explore these and other significant models, unraveling their stories and understanding their impact on the brands' legacies.

Brand ambassadors and partnerships:

Brand ambassadors and strategic partnerships have long played a significant role in enhancing the reputation and desirability of vintage watch brands. These collaborations bring together the worlds of horology, art, sports, and entertainment, creating powerful associations that resonate with collectors and enthusiasts. Let's explore some notable brand ambassadors and partnerships that have contributed to the allure of Rolex, Omega, Patek Philippe, and Audemars Piguet.

Rolex:

Rolex and Motorsports: Rolex has a strong association with motorsports, particularly in the world of endurance racing and Formula 1. Through partnerships with iconic races like the 24 Hours of Le Mans and legendary drivers like Sir Jackie Stewart and Ayrton Senna, Rolex has solidified its connection with precision, performance, and timeless elegance.

Rolex and Exploration: Rolex has a rich history of supporting explorers and adventurers. From sponsoring the historic Everest expedition to partnering with organizations like National Geographic and the National Geographic Society, Rolex celebrates those who push the boundaries of human achievement.

Omega:

Omega and Space Exploration: Omega's association with space exploration is legendary. As the official timekeeper of NASA, Omega's Speedmaster Professional became the watch of choice for astronauts during the Apollo missions, earning it the nickname "Moonwatch." The partnership between Omega and space exploration continues to inspire and captivate watch enthusiasts.

Omega and Olympic Games: Omega has been the official timekeeper of the Olympic Games for decades. This enduring partnership highlights the brand's commitment to precision and accuracy, as well as its dedication to the celebration of human achievement in sports.

Patek Philippe:

Patek Philippe and Arts: Patek Philippe has fostered strong connections with the arts and cultural institutions. The brand has collaborated with renowned artists, designers, and architects, supporting initiatives that celebrate creativity and craftsmanship. These partnerships highlight the brand's commitment to timeless beauty and artistic excellence.

Patek Philippe and Philanthropy: Patek Philippe has been actively involved in philanthropic endeavors, supporting causes related to healthcare, education, and cultural heritage. Through partnerships with organizations like the Children's Medical Research Foundation and the Louvre Museum, Patek Philippe showcases its commitment to making a positive impact on society.

Audemars Piguet:

Audemars Piguet and Sports: Audemars Piguet has forged strong relationships with various sports disciplines. The brand has collaborated with legendary golfers like Rory McIlroy and Serena Williams, emphasizing the shared values of precision, performance, and innovation.

Audemars Piguet and Art: Audemars Piguet has a deep appreciation for art and creativity, reflected in its partnerships with renowned artists, designers, and art institutions. Collaborations such as the "Art Basel" and the "Audemars Piguet

Art Commission" demonstrate the brand's commitment to pushing boundaries and exploring new artistic expressions.

These brand ambassadors and partnerships have not only added to the mystique and desirability of vintage watch brands but have also reinforced their values, aesthetics, and commitment to excellence. By aligning themselves with influential personalities, notable events, and meaningful causes, Rolex, Omega, Patek Philippe, and Audemars Piguet have created powerful connections that resonate with collectors and enthusiasts, further enhancing the appeal of their vintage timepieces.

Collectibility and investment potential of vintage watch brands:

Rarity and collectibility:

One of the key factors that contribute to the value and desirability of vintage watches is their rarity. Within the realms of Rolex, Omega, Patek Philippe, and Audemars Piguet, there are specific models that hold an esteemed status among collectors due to their limited production numbers, unique features, or historical significance. Let's explore some of these rare and sought-after vintage models from each brand:

Rolex:

Rolex Daytona "Paul Newman": The Rolex Daytona with the exotic "Paul Newman" dial has become one of the most coveted vintage watches in the world. Produced in limited quantities during the 1960s and 1970s, these models feature a distinct dial design with artful subdials and unique font styles. Their scarcity and association with the iconic actor and racing enthusiast Paul Newman have propelled their collectibility and market value to extraordinary heights.

Rolex Submariner "Double Red Sea-Dweller": The Rolex Submariner "Double Red Sea-Dweller" is a highly sought-after vintage model known for its distinctive dial featuring two lines of red text. Produced for a relatively short period in the late 1960s and early 1970s, these watches were designed for professional divers and are prized for their rarity, robustness, and historical significance in Rolex's dive watch lineage.

Omega:

Omega Speedmaster Professional "Apollo 11 50th Anniversary": Released in 2019 to commemorate the 50th anniversary of the Apollo 11 moon landing, this limited-edition Omega Speedmaster Professional pays homage to the original Moonwatch worn by astronauts. With its unique design elements, such as a moon crater motif on the dial and a caseback featuring the lunar surface, this model holds immense collectibility for space and watch enthusiasts alike.

Omega Seamaster 300 "Big Triangle": The Omega Seamaster 300 "Big Triangle" is a vintage diver's watch that features a large luminous triangle at the 12 o'clock position on the dial. Produced in the 1960s, these watches are highly sought after due to their distinctive design, limited production numbers, and association with Omega's rich diving heritage.

Patek Philippe:

Patek Philippe Nautilus: The Patek Philippe Nautilus, introduced in 1976, is an iconic luxury sports watch that has gained legendary status among collectors. With its distinctive porthole-inspired design and high-quality craftsmanship, the Nautilus is known for its exclusivity and limited production numbers, making certain models, such as the reference 5711, highly sought after in the vintage watch market.

Patek Philippe Calatrava "Clous de Paris": The Patek Philippe Calatrava collection includes various models adorned with the intricate "Clous de Paris" guilloché pattern on the dial. These timepieces, known for their elegant simplicity and timeless appeal, hold collectible value due to their scarcity and the exceptional craftsmanship associated with the Patek Philippe brand.

Audemars Piguet:

Audemars Piguet Royal Oak "A-Series": The Audemars Piguet Royal Oak, designed by Gerald Genta, revolutionized the concept of luxury sports watches when it was introduced in 1972. The earliest versions, known as the "A-Series," are particularly prized by collectors due to their historical significance and limited production numbers. These watches represent a defining moment in Audemars Piguet's history and hold significant collectibility.

Audemars Piguet Royal Oak Offshore "End of Days": The Audemars Piguet Royal Oak Offshore "End of Days" is a highly sought-after limited-edition model that gained popularity after it was featured in the movie "End of Days" starring Arnold Schwarzenegger. With its unique black and yellow accents, this watch holds collectible value for both Audemars Piguet enthusiasts and movie memorabilia collectors.

These examples represent just a fraction of the rare and sought-after vintage models that have captivated watch collectors. Whether it's the limited production numbers, unique features, or historical context, these timepieces embody the essence of rarity and hold immense collectibility within the vintage watch market. Owning such a piece allows collectors to not only possess a remarkable timekeeping instrument but also a tangible piece of horological history.

Market demand and pricing trends:

The vintage watch market is a dynamic and ever-evolving landscape where market demand and pricing trends play a significant role in shaping the value and collectibility of timepieces. When it comes to renowned brands like Rolex, Omega, Patek Philippe, and Audemars Piguet, the market dynamics are particularly intriguing. Let's delve into the current market trends, auction records, and factors driving the demand and pricing of vintage watches from these esteemed brands:

Rolex:

Rolex holds a strong position in the vintage watch market, with a reputation for exceptional quality, enduring designs, and an avid collector base. Demand for vintage Rolex watches remains high, with iconic models such as the Submariner, Daytona, and GMT-Master commanding significant attention and value. Factors driving the demand include their timeless design, historical significance, and association with notable individuals or events.

In recent years, vintage Rolex watches have experienced substantial price increases, driven by factors such as scarcity, desirability, and the brand's consistent popularity. Auction records have witnessed remarkable prices achieved for rare and exceptional Rolex models, often surpassing their pre-sale estimates. The market demand for vintage Rolex watches is fueled by a mix of passionate collectors, investors seeking alternative assets, and enthusiasts drawn to the allure of horological history.

Omega:

The vintage Omega watch market has witnessed notable growth and increased interest in recent years. Vintage Omega models, particularly those associated with space exploration, such as the Speedmaster Professional worn during the Apollo moon missions, are highly sought after by collectors. The historical significance of these watches, coupled with Omega's reputation for precision and craftsmanship, has propelled their demand and pricing.

Auction records have highlighted the increasing value of vintage Omega watches, with rare and well-preserved examples achieving impressive results. The demand for vintage Omega timepieces is influenced by factors such as their association with significant historical events, the brand's commitment to innovation, and the enduring appeal of their classic designs.

Patek Philippe:

Patek Philippe holds a revered position in the world of horology, and vintage Patek Philippe watches are coveted by collectors for their exceptional craftsmanship, timeless designs, and limited production numbers. The brand's reputation for precision and complicated movements, coupled with its heritage and prestigious lineage, contribute to the strong market demand and pricing of vintage Patek Philippe timepieces.

Auction records consistently demonstrate the exceptional value placed on vintage Patek Philippe watches, particularly rare and important models such as complicated complications, unique dials, or significant historical provenance. The enduring popularity of Patek Philippe, coupled with its unwavering commitment to craftsmanship and exclusivity, ensures a sustained demand for vintage examples in the market.

Audemars Piguet:

Audemars Piguet has established itself as a brand synonymous with luxury and innovation, and vintage Audemars Piguet watches hold a special place in the hearts of collectors. The demand for vintage Audemars Piguet timepieces, particularly the iconic Royal Oak collection, remains strong. The Royal Oak's avant-garde design, Gerald Genta's visionary creation, has become a hallmark of the brand and continues to resonate with watch enthusiasts.

Auction records illustrate the desirability and robust pricing of vintage Audemars Piguet watches, especially limited-edition models or those associated with notable partnerships and collaborations. The demand for vintage Audemars Piguet timepieces is fueled by their distinctive design, exceptional craftsmanship, and the brand's ability to balance tradition and innovation.

The vintage watch market for Rolex, Omega, Patek Philippe, and Audemars Piguet is characterized by robust demand, appreciating prices, and a passionate collector base. Factors such as brand reputation, historical significance, scarcity, and the enduring appeal of iconic models contribute to the strong market dynamics and pricing trends. Whether as a passionate collector or an astute investor, navigating these market trends and understanding the factors driving demand can enhance one's appreciation and success in the vintage watch market.

Investment considerations:

Investing in vintage watches from established brands like Rolex, Omega, Patek Philippe, and Audemars Piguet requires careful consideration of various factors to make informed investment decisions. Let's explore some key investment considerations when delving into the vintage watch market:

Market fluctuations:

The vintage watch market, like any investment market, experiences fluctuations in demand and pricing. It's important to stay updated on market trends, auction results, and the overall sentiment of collectors and enthusiasts. This information can provide insights into the market's health, identify emerging trends, and help anticipate potential fluctuations in value.

Authenticity verification:

The vintage watch market is not immune to the presence of counterfeit or altered timepieces. Authenticity verification is crucial to ensure that the watch you are considering for investment is genuine and retains its original components. Working with reputable dealers, experts, or authentication services can help authenticate the vintage watch and provide peace of mind.

Rarity and condition:

Rarity and condition play a significant role in the value and investment potential of vintage watches. Limited production numbers, discontinued models, or unique variations often command higher prices due to their scarcity. Additionally, watches in excellent condition, with original components and minimal restoration, tend to be more desirable among collectors. Assessing the rarity and condition of a vintage watch is essential when evaluating its investment potential.

Historical significance and provenance:

Vintage watches with notable historical significance or compelling provenance can fetch higher prices and attract passionate collectors. Consider watches associated with important events, famous owners, or specific periods in horological history. The story and heritage behind a vintage watch can enhance its desirability and long-term investment prospects.

Growth prospects:

Evaluating the growth prospects of vintage watches involves understanding factors that contribute to their appreciation in value over time. This includes studying historical price trends, assessing the demand for specific models or brands, and staying informed about industry developments. Vintage watches with strong track records of appreciation and a continued interest among collectors may present favorable growth prospects for investment.

Maintenance and servicing:

Proper maintenance and servicing are essential for preserving the value and longevity of vintage watches. Regular servicing by experienced watchmakers can help ensure the watch functions optimally and retains its condition. Considering the availability of spare parts and access to reliable servicing options is crucial when investing in vintage watches.

Portfolio diversification:

Vintage watches can be a valuable addition to an investment portfolio, but it's important to maintain diversification. Balancing vintage watch investments with other asset classes can help mitigate risks and optimize overall portfolio performance. Diversification can involve spreading investments across different brands, models, price ranges, or even including modern watches to capture both historical and contemporary market trends.

Long-term perspective:

Investing in vintage watches requires a long-term perspective. While short-term fluctuations in the market may occur, the potential for value appreciation over time is often realized with patient and informed investment strategies. Vintage watches can offer unique investment opportunities for those who appreciate the craftsmanship, heritage, and aesthetic appeal of these timepieces.

Investing in vintage watches from established brands requires careful consideration of market fluctuations, authenticity verification, rarity, condition, historical significance, growth prospects, maintenance, portfolio diversification, and a long-term perspective. By conducting thorough research, seeking expert advice, and staying informed about the market, investors can make informed decisions and potentially benefit from the appreciation and allure of vintage timepieces.

Expert tips and resources for exploring vintage watch brands:

Research and resources:

Books:
There are several authoritative books written by horological experts that delve into the history, models, and intricacies of vintage watches. Look for titles such as "Vintage Rolex: The Largest Collection in the World" by Guido Mondani, "Moonwatch Only: The Ultimate Omega Speedmaster Guide" by Grégoire Rossier and Anthony Marquié, "Patek Philippe: The Authorized Biography" by Nicholas Foulkes, and "Audemars Piguet: Masterpieces of Time" by Florence Müller.

Online platforms and forums:
The internet provides a wealth of information and platforms dedicated to vintage watches. Websites like Hodinkee, WatchTime, and Fratello Watches offer comprehensive articles, reviews, and insights into vintage watch brands. Additionally, enthusiast forums such as Watchuseek and TimeZone provide spaces for discussions, questions, and sharing experiences with fellow collectors.

Auction houses:
Major auction houses like Christie's, Sotheby's, and Phillips host regular watch auctions that feature exceptional vintage timepieces. These auctions are not only opportunities to acquire vintage watches but also valuable resources for studying market trends, historical prices, and the authenticity of specific models. Auction house catalogs and online archives can serve as valuable reference materials for collectors and investors.

Vintage watch dealers and experts:
Building relationships with reputable vintage watch dealers and experts is essential for gaining insights and access to authentic vintage watches. Seek out established dealers who specialize in vintage watches and have a track record of expertise and integrity. They can provide guidance, share their knowledge, and assist in sourcing desirable vintage models.

Horological museums and exhibitions:

Visiting horological museums and exhibitions can be an enriching experience to deepen your understanding of vintage watch brands. Museums such as the Patek Philippe Museum in Geneva, the Omega Museum in Switzerland, and the Audemars Piguet Museum in Le Brassus offer an opportunity to appreciate rare vintage watches, understand the brands' heritage, and learn about significant horological milestones.

Collector communities and events:

Engaging with collector communities and attending watch events can provide valuable networking opportunities and access to a wealth of knowledge. Joining watch collector groups, attending watch fairs, or participating in meetups allows you to connect with like-minded individuals, share experiences, and gain insights from seasoned collectors.

Expert appraisals and authentication services:

When considering high-value vintage watches, expert appraisals and authentication services can provide professional evaluations and ensure the authenticity and condition of the timepiece. Seek out trusted horological experts or reputable authentication services that specialize in vintage watches.

While these resources can provide valuable information, it's important to approach vintage watch exploration with a discerning eye, conduct thorough research, and seek multiple sources of information. Developing a well-rounded understanding of vintage watch brands requires a combination of studying historical records, engaging with experts and enthusiasts, and immersing yourself in the world of horology.

Authenticity verification:

Authenticity verification is crucial when it comes to vintage watches, as the market is unfortunately plagued with counterfeit or modified timepieces. Here are some tips and recommended methods for verifying the authenticity of vintage watches:

Research and reference materials:

Familiarize yourself with the specific brand's historical records, production details, and serial number ranges. Brands like Rolex and Omega have comprehensive databases available online, allowing you to check the authenticity of a watch by entering its serial number and other relevant details. Additionally, reference books and reputable online resources can provide valuable information about authentic features, dial variations, case markings, and other distinguishing characteristics of vintage watches.

Serial numbers and hallmarks:

Vintage watches often have unique serial numbers engraved on the case or movement. Research the appropriate serial number ranges for specific models and compare them to the watch you're examining. In addition, familiarize yourself with the hallmarks or stamps that indicate the watch's country of origin, material quality, and other relevant details. This information can help you identify inconsistencies or discrepancies that may raise concerns about authenticity.

Examination of components:

Carefully examine the watch's components, such as the dial, hands, case, crown, and movement. Look for signs of originality, such as matching patina, correct logos or engravings, and appropriate branding. Any inconsistencies, such as incorrect fonts, misaligned markings, or poor craftsmanship, could indicate a potential counterfeit or modified watch. It's important to compare the watch to authentic reference models or seek the opinion of trusted experts for a thorough evaluation.

Consult with experts:

When in doubt, seek the advice of experienced vintage watch experts, horologists, or authorized dealers specializing in the particular brand or model you're interested in. Their expertise and knowledge of the nuances of vintage watches can help you identify potential red flags and provide professional opinions on authenticity. Experts can also assist with authentication certificates or historical documentation, which can add credibility to the vintage timepiece.

Physical examination and movement inspection:

If possible, have a trained watchmaker or expert examine the watch in person. They can assess the movement's quality, authenticity, and condition, as well as verify the presence of appropriate manufacturer's marks or signatures. A thorough inspection can help identify any signs of tampering, replacement parts, or other modifications that may impact the watch's authenticity.

Purchase from reputable sources:

To minimize the risk of purchasing counterfeit or misrepresented vintage watches, it's advisable to buy from established, reputable sources. Authorized dealers, renowned auction houses, and trusted vintage watch dealers with a proven track record of authenticity and customer satisfaction are recommended. These sources often have stringent authentication processes in place and provide guarantees or certifications of authenticity.

While these methods can assist in verifying the authenticity of vintage watches, they may not provide definitive proof in all cases. Counterfeiters are becoming increasingly sophisticated, making it essential to combine multiple verification methods, conduct thorough research, and seek expert opinions when necessary. Being cautious, knowledgeable, and diligent in your authentication process will help ensure that you are acquiring genuine vintage timepieces for your collection.

Building a vintage watch collection:

Building a vintage watch collection can be a rewarding and exciting endeavor. Here are some tips to help you build a diverse and well-curated vintage watch collection:

Define your collecting goals:

Start by defining your collecting goals and preferences. Determine if you have a specific focus, such as collecting watches from a particular era, brand, or complication. Consider your budget, personal style, and the story you want your collection to tell. Having a clear vision will guide your decisions and help you build a collection that reflects your unique tastes and interests.

Research and expand your knowledge:

Take the time to research and educate yourself about different vintage watch brands, models, and historical significance. Read books, browse online forums and communities, and engage with experienced collectors to learn from their insights. Building your knowledge will enable you to make informed decisions and identify valuable timepieces.

Seek variety and balance:

Aim for diversity in your collection by including watches from different brands, models, and price ranges. This diversity not only adds visual interest but also minimizes the risk of overexposure to a single brand or style. Explore watches from both well-known brands and lesser-known or niche brands to discover hidden gems and unique pieces that resonate with your collecting goals.

Condition and originality:

Pay attention to the condition and originality of the watches you consider adding to your collection. Well-preserved vintage watches in original condition tend to hold higher value and appeal to collectors. Look for watches with minimal signs of wear, unpolished cases, and original components whenever possible. However, keep in mind that some vintage watches may require minor restoration or servicing to ensure optimal functionality.

Price range and budgeting:

Determine your budget and allocate funds accordingly. Vintage watches can vary significantly in price, and it's essential to set realistic expectations based on your financial capabilities. Consider starting with more accessible price ranges and gradually expanding your collection as your budget allows. Remember that value can be found at various price points, and the enjoyment of collecting is not solely dependent on the cost of the watches.

Seek trusted sellers and experts:

When purchasing vintage watches, it's crucial to buy from reputable sellers and experts in the field. Look for trusted vintage watch dealers, auction houses with a track record of integrity, or authorized dealers specializing in vintage timepieces. These sources can provide authentication, offer warranties or guarantees, and ensure a smooth buying experience.

Curate with passion and personal taste:

Ultimately, building a vintage watch collection is a personal journey driven by passion. Let your personal taste and instinct guide your choices. Curate a collection that speaks to you and reflects your unique style. Each watch should have a story or meaning that resonates with you, whether it's a historical significance, an exceptional design, or a personal connection.

Regularly evaluate and refine your collection:

As you continue to build your vintage watch collection, periodically evaluate and refine it. Assess if the watches align with your collecting goals and if any adjustments or additions are needed to maintain a well-balanced and cohesive collection. Selling or trading watches that no longer align with your vision can free up resources for acquiring new additions that better fit your evolving preferences.

Building a vintage watch collection is a journey that requires patience, research, and an appreciation for the art and history of timepieces. Enjoy the process, celebrate each addition to your collection, and share your passion with fellow collectors.

Part 3: Investing in Old Watch Brands

Vintage watches not only hold historical and sentimental value but also present an intriguing investment opportunity. In this section, we will uncover the strategies, considerations, and insights necessary for making informed investment decisions in old watch brands. From renowned luxury brands with rich heritage to regional or niche brands with unique value propositions, we will delve into each brand's development, market trends, and investment potential.

Join us as we navigate the world of vintage watch investing, discovering the allure of vintage watch collecting, exploring the significance of established luxury brands, and uncovering the charm of regional and niche brands. We will discuss rarity and scarcity, historical context and provenance, design and aesthetics, collector preferences and trends, collecting strategies, preservation and restoration, investment considerations, and expert tips and resources for exploring vintage watch brands. Prepare to embark on an exciting journey of vintage watch investment and uncover the possibilities that lie within this captivating world.

Understanding the investment potential of vintage watch brands:

Historical appreciation:

Historical appreciation is a key aspect of investing in vintage watches. Certain brands have demonstrated a consistent track record of value appreciation over the years, making them attractive options for investors. Understanding the historical appreciation of vintage watches can provide valuable insights into their investment potential.

One notable example of historical appreciation is the Rolex Daytona. Originally introduced in the 1960s, the Daytona struggled initially to gain popularity. However, over time, the Daytona became highly sought after, especially the vintage models from the 1960s and 1970s. These vintage Daytonas, with their manual-winding movements and exotic dials, have seen significant price increases in the market. For instance, the Rolex Daytona "Paul Newman" models, named after the iconic actor and race car driver, have achieved astronomical prices at auctions, with some models reaching millions of dollars.

Another brand that has experienced historical appreciation is Patek Philippe. Known for their exquisite craftsmanship and complicated movements, vintage Patek Philippe watches have consistently gained value. Notable examples include the Patek Philippe Calatrava Ref. 570, which has seen steady price appreciation over the years. Vintage Patek Philippe chronograph models, such as the Ref. 1463 and Ref. 130, have also witnessed significant price increases due to their rarity and desirability among collectors.

Omega Speedmaster watches, especially those with historical significance, have also shown remarkable appreciation. The Omega Speedmaster Professional Moonwatch, famously worn by astronauts during the Apollo missions, has become an iconic timepiece with a strong collector following. Vintage models from the 1960s, particularly those with the coveted "Pre-Moon" designation, have experienced substantial price growth. The rarity and historical significance of these watches have contributed to their appreciation in value over time.

It is important to note that historical appreciation may vary across different models, editions, and conditions. Factors such as scarcity, desirability, condition, and historical significance play a significant role in determining the extent of price appreciation. Conducting thorough research, consulting experts, and staying informed about market trends are crucial in identifying vintage watches with a history of appreciation and potential for future growth.

While historical appreciation is not guaranteed for every vintage watch, studying the market trends and understanding the factors that contribute to price increases can assist investors in making informed decisions. It is essential to consider the brand's reputation, historical significance, rarity, and demand among collectors when evaluating the potential for historical appreciation in vintage watches. By leveraging this knowledge, investors can navigate the vintage watch market with confidence and increase their chances of achieving substantial returns on their investments.

Rarity and collectibility:

Rarity and collectibility are crucial factors that contribute to the investment potential of vintage watches from renowned brands. The scarcity of certain models, limited editions, and unique variations significantly enhances their desirability among collectors, driving up their value in the market.

Many vintage watches from established brands are sought after due to their limited production numbers. Manufacturers often release limited editions or special models that are produced in small quantities, making them rare and highly coveted. For example, Rolex has released various limited-edition watches over the years, such as the "Paul Newman" Daytona or the "Milsub" Submariner, which were produced in limited numbers and are now highly collectible. The scarcity of these models, coupled with their historical significance and unique features, increases their investment potential.

Specific models within a brand's lineup can also exhibit rarity and collectibility. Certain vintage watches gain prominence due to their unique design, significant historical context, or specific features. These models often have a limited production run, making them harder to find in the market. For instance, the Omega Speedmaster "Ed White" reference 105.003, known for being the first Speedmaster worn in space, holds immense collectible value due to its historical significance and limited availability. Similarly, Patek Philippe's reference 2499, a highly complicated and rare perpetual calendar chronograph, is highly sought after by collectors.

Limited production numbers and specific models contribute to the exclusivity and collectibility of vintage watches, which in turn drives their investment potential. Collectors are willing to pay a premium for these rare timepieces, especially when they are in excellent condition and accompanied by proper documentation.

It is important to note that rarity alone does not guarantee investment success. Factors such as the overall condition of the watch, its originality, historical significance, and demand among collectors all play a role in determining its investment potential. Thorough research and expert advice are crucial in assessing the rarity and collectibility of vintage watches from different brands. By understanding the market demand and the factors that contribute to their scarcity, investors can make informed decisions and pursue opportunities that align with their investment goals.

Investing in rare and collectible vintage watches requires careful consideration and due diligence. It is essential to stay informed about market trends, track auction results, and seek expert opinions to assess the investment potential of specific models or limited editions. By leveraging the rarity and collectibility of vintage watches from established brands, investors can tap into a market that offers both the joy of collecting and the potential for significant financial returns.

Brand reputation and desirability:

Brand reputation and desirability play a significant role in the investment appeal of vintage watches. Established vintage watch brands with a strong reputation and heritage have built a loyal following and garnered a high level of desirability among collectors and enthusiasts. Here, we explore how brand reputation and desirability contribute to the investment appeal of vintage watches.

Heritage and Legacy: Vintage watch brands with a long and illustrious history have established a reputation for craftsmanship, quality, and innovation over the years. These brands have a track record of producing timepieces that stand the test of time and retain their value. For example, brands like Rolex, Omega, Patek Philippe, and Audemars Piguet have been at the forefront of watchmaking for decades, consistently delivering exceptional watches that command respect and admiration.

Craftsmanship and Quality: Vintage watches from reputable brands are known for their meticulous craftsmanship, attention to detail, and high-quality materials. These watches are often crafted by skilled artisans using traditional techniques, resulting in timepieces of exceptional quality and enduring value. Collectors appreciate the fine craftsmanship and superior build quality of vintage watches, making them highly desirable in the market.

Iconic Designs and Timeless Appeal: Vintage watches from renowned brands often feature iconic designs that have stood the test of time and remain highly sought after. These designs have become synonymous with the brand's identity and are instantly recognizable to collectors. The enduring appeal of these iconic designs contributes to the desirability and investment potential of vintage watches.

Limited Availability: Vintage watches from reputable brands are often limited in availability, especially when it comes to older models or discontinued references. This limited supply adds to their desirability and drives up their value in the market. Collectors and investors recognize the scarcity of these vintage timepieces, making them highly sought after and prized additions to any collection.

Resale Value and Market Demand: Vintage watches from esteemed brands have demonstrated a consistent and strong resale value over time. Their desirability among collectors and the wider market ensures a healthy demand, which contributes to their investment appeal. These watches have proven to hold their value well and, in many cases, appreciate over time, making them attractive options for investors looking for long-term growth.

Brand reputation and desirability create a sense of trust and confidence in vintage watch investments. Collectors and investors are drawn to the rich heritage, exceptional craftsmanship, and timeless appeal of vintage watches from renowned brands. The reputation of these brands provides assurance that the watches have been produced to the highest standards and will continue to be valued by collectors in the future.

It's important to note that brand reputation alone should not be the sole basis for investment decisions. Other factors such as the condition of the watch, its historical significance, and market trends should also be considered. Conducting thorough research, seeking expert advice, and staying informed about the vintage watch market are essential steps in maximizing the investment potential of vintage watches from reputable brands.

Factors to consider when investing in old watch brands:

Condition and authenticity:

Condition and authenticity are crucial factors to consider when investing in vintage watches. Acquiring a vintage watch in good condition and ensuring its authenticity are essential for both the enjoyment of owning a timepiece and the preservation of its investment value. Here, we emphasize the significance of condition and authenticity and provide guidance on how to assess them.

Condition:

The condition of a vintage watch greatly impacts its value and desirability. A well-preserved watch with minimal signs of wear, a clean dial, intact components, and a fully functioning movement is highly sought after by collectors. Watches in excellent condition often command higher prices and are more likely to appreciate in value over time. On the other hand, watches with significant damage, excessive wear, or missing parts may have lower investment potential.

To evaluate the condition of a vintage watch, it is important to consider factors such as:

- Case condition: Look for scratches, dents, or signs of polishing that may affect the watch's originality and value.
- Dial condition: Assess the dial for discoloration, fading, or damage, as these can significantly impact the watch's appeal.
- Hands and markers: Check the hands and markers for any damage, corrosion, or mismatched replacements.
- Movement: Ensure that the movement is in good working order and has been properly serviced or restored.

Authenticity:

Authenticity verification is crucial to ensure that the vintage watch is a genuine piece produced by the brand it claims to be. Counterfeit watches and fraudulent modifications can be common in the vintage watch market, so conducting thorough research and seeking expert verification is essential.

To verify the authenticity of a vintage watch, consider the following:

- Research: Gather information about the specific model, its features, and production details. Consult reputable sources, reference books, and online forums dedicated to vintage watches.
- Serial numbers and markings: Check the watch's serial numbers, hallmarks, and other identifying marks to ensure they align with the brand's records and historical data.
- Expert verification: Consult experts, watchmakers, or experienced collectors who specialize in vintage watches. They can provide insights and expertise to help authenticate the watch based on their knowledge and experience.
- Documentation and provenance: Look for any accompanying documentation, such as original papers, warranty cards, or service records. Provenance, including information about previous owners or historical significance, can also support the authenticity of a vintage watch.
-

Investing in a vintage watch with a good condition and verified authenticity not only enhances the watch's value but also provides peace of mind to the collector or investor. It is crucial to approach vintage watch acquisition with diligence, conducting thorough research, seeking expert advice, and ensuring proper verification to make informed investment decisions.

By prioritizing condition and authenticity, collectors can build a portfolio of vintage watches that not only showcases exceptional craftsmanship and design but also holds strong investment potential over the long term.

Market trends and demand:

Staying informed about market trends and understanding collector preferences and shifts in demand is vital for vintage watch investors. The vintage watch market is dynamic and influenced by various factors, including evolving tastes, emerging trends, and changing economic conditions. Here, we delve into the significance of monitoring market trends and demand and how it can assist investors in making informed decisions.

Market trends:

Keeping a pulse on market trends allows investors to identify patterns and fluctuations that can impact the value and demand for vintage watches. By staying informed, investors can make better decisions regarding which brands, models, or specific time periods to focus on. Some key aspects to consider include:

- Popular brands and models: Recognizing the brands and models that are currently in high demand among collectors can help investors target watches with strong potential for appreciation.
- Design trends: Understanding design trends can help investors identify watches that align with current aesthetic preferences. Certain design elements, such as specific dial configurations, bezel styles, or case materials, may experience increased demand in the market.
- Emerging trends: Being aware of emerging trends in the vintage watch market allows investors to identify opportunities before they become mainstream. This could involve recognizing the growing popularity of particular brands, models, or design eras that are currently undervalued but have the potential for future appreciation.

Collector preferences:

Collector preferences play a significant role in shaping market demand for vintage watches. Collector tastes and preferences can evolve over time, with certain brands or models experiencing surges in popularity. Understanding collector preferences can help investors anticipate which watches are likely to be in high demand and adjust their investment strategy accordingly. Some key considerations include:

- Design aesthetics: Certain design styles or eras may be favored by collectors, such as the sleek and sporty designs of the 1960s or the bold and robust styles of the 1970s.
- Complications and features: Vintage watches with unique complications or innovative features, such as chronographs, moon phases, or GMT functions, often attract collector interest.
- Historical significance: Watches associated with historical events, famous personalities, or significant milestones in watchmaking history tend to garner heightened collector attention.

By staying informed about market trends and collector preferences, investors can make well-informed decisions about which vintage watches to acquire or hold in their portfolio. Monitoring market trends can help investors identify opportunities, capitalize on emerging trends, and avoid potential pitfalls.

It's important to note that while market trends and demand are valuable indicators, they should not be the sole basis for investment decisions. Investors should also consider their own investment goals, risk tolerance, and personal preferences when building a vintage watch portfolio.

By combining market insights with a comprehensive understanding of the vintage watch market, investors can make informed decisions, optimize their investment strategy, and maximize the potential for long-term returns.

Historical significance and cultural value:

The historical significance and cultural value associated with vintage watches from renowned brands play a crucial role in their investment potential. These factors contribute to the desirability and allure of certain watches among collectors and enthusiasts. Here, we delve into the importance of historical significance and cultural value in vintage watch investments.

Historical events:

Vintage watches that have a connection to significant historical events often hold a special place in the market. For example, timepieces worn by historical figures, used in explorations or expeditions, or linked to notable achievements in sports or aviation can carry a unique historical significance. The association with such events adds a layer of storytelling and intrigue to the watch, enhancing its desirability and value.

Cultural relevance:

Vintage watches often embody the cultural spirit of their respective eras. They reflect the prevailing trends, design philosophies, and societal values of the time. These watches serve as artifacts of cultural history, capturing the essence of specific periods and influencing the evolution of watchmaking. Watches that epitomize the design language and spirit of a particular era, such as the Art Deco period of the 1920s or the Space Age aesthetics of the 1960s, hold cultural value and attract collectors who appreciate the historical context.

Iconic design elements:

Vintage watches are revered for their iconic design elements that have stood the test of time. Certain brands have introduced design innovations or distinctive features that have become synonymous with their identity. These design elements can include specific case shapes, bezel designs, dial configurations, or bracelet styles. Watches that possess these iconic design elements are highly sought after by collectors and enthusiasts, driving their investment potential.

The historical significance and cultural value associated with vintage watches create a sense of narrative and emotional connection for collectors. Owning a watch with ties to significant events or cultural movements allows collectors to own a piece of history and become custodians of cultural heritage.

Investors who recognize the historical and cultural importance of vintage watches can strategically select timepieces that possess these qualities. Such watches often have enduring appeal and are more likely to hold their value or appreciate over time. However, it is essential to conduct thorough research and ensure the authenticity and provenance of the watches to fully capitalize on their historical significance and cultural value.

By understanding the historical context, cultural relevance, and iconic design elements of vintage watches, investors can make informed decisions about which timepieces to include in their portfolios. This knowledge enables them to appreciate the narrative behind each watch and recognize the broader cultural and historical significance that contributes to their investment potential.

Strategies for investing in old watch brands:

Portfolio diversification:

Portfolio diversification is a fundamental principle of investment, and it holds true when it comes to vintage watch investments as well. Diversifying a vintage watch portfolio involves including timepieces from different brands, eras, and price points. Here, we explore the benefits of portfolio diversification in vintage watch investing.

Risk mitigation:
Diversification helps mitigate risk by spreading investments across different assets. In the context of vintage watches, including watches from various brands and eras can help balance the inherent risks associated with individual brands or specific models. By diversifying, investors reduce their exposure to any one brand's fluctuations in value, production challenges, or changing market trends. A diversified portfolio helps cushion against potential losses and provides stability.

Maximizing growth opportunities:
Investing in vintage watches from different brands and eras allows investors to capitalize on various growth opportunities. Different brands may experience fluctuations in popularity and market demand at different times. By diversifying, investors can potentially benefit from the appreciation of watches from multiple brands simultaneously. Additionally, including watches from different eras allows investors to capture the unique appeal and market potential of specific time periods.

Preservation of capital:
Vintage watches, like any other investment, carry a certain level of market risk. Diversifying a vintage watch portfolio helps protect capital by reducing the impact of any single watch's decline in value. Even if one watch underperforms, the overall portfolio can remain relatively stable or experience growth through

the performance of other watches. This preservation of capital is crucial for long-term investment success.

Enhanced liquidity:

Diversifying a vintage watch portfolio can also enhance liquidity. While some watches may have high demand and attract buyers quickly, others may take longer to sell. By including watches from different brands, eras, and price points, investors have a greater likelihood of finding buyers in various market segments. This diversification ensures a more balanced liquidity profile and reduces reliance on the sale of a single watch to generate cash flow.

Collecting opportunities and enjoyment:

Diversifying a vintage watch portfolio allows investors to explore a wide range of brands, models, and design aesthetics. It offers the opportunity to appreciate the unique characteristics and craftsmanship of watches from different eras and makers. The process of building a diverse collection can be enjoyable and intellectually stimulating for watch enthusiasts, adding a personal dimension to the investment journey.

When diversifying a vintage watch portfolio, it is essential to consider factors such as brand reputation, market demand, historical significance, and investment potential. By carefully selecting watches from different brands, eras, and price points, investors can achieve a balanced and well-rounded vintage watch portfolio that maximizes growth potential, mitigates risk, and provides an enjoyable collecting experience.

Buy-and-hold approach:

The buy-and-hold approach is a long-term investment strategy that involves acquiring vintage watches from established brands and holding onto them for an extended period with the expectation of capital appreciation over time. Here, we delve into the advantages of adopting a buy-and-hold approach when investing in vintage watches from these renowned brands.

Capital appreciation potential:

Vintage watches from established brands have a track record of appreciating in value over the long term. By adopting a buy-and-hold strategy, investors can benefit from the potential for significant capital appreciation as the watches become scarcer and more sought after. As time goes by, the historical significance, craftsmanship, and desirability of these watches tend to increase, contributing to their value appreciation.

Weathering market fluctuations:

Vintage watch markets, like any investment market, can experience short-term fluctuations and volatility. By adopting a buy-and-hold strategy, investors can weather these ups and downs without being influenced by short-term market noise. Holding onto watches from established brands allows investors to take a long-term view and ride out market fluctuations, ultimately benefiting from the overall growth trajectory of the vintage watch market.

Preservation of historical and cultural value:

Vintage watches from these established brands carry significant historical and cultural value. By holding onto these watches, investors contribute to the preservation and appreciation of horological heritage. As time passes, the historical significance and craftsmanship of these watches become increasingly valued, making them sought after by collectors and enthusiasts. By holding onto vintage watches, investors play a role in preserving these timepieces as cultural artifacts.

Opportunity for compounding returns:

The buy-and-hold strategy allows investors to benefit from the power of compounding returns. As vintage watches appreciate in value over time, the initial investment can grow exponentially. By reinvesting the proceeds from the sale of other watches or using the accumulated capital gains to acquire additional vintage watches, investors can further enhance their returns through compounding. This long-term compounding effect can significantly contribute to overall investment success.

Reduced transaction costs and taxes:

The buy-and-hold approach minimizes transaction costs and potential tax implications associated with frequent buying and selling of vintage watches. By holding onto the watches for the long term, investors avoid incurring transaction fees, commissions, and taxes associated with frequent trading. This cost-saving aspect of the buy-and-hold strategy allows investors to maximize their investment returns.

It's important to note that a successful buy-and-hold strategy requires careful selection of vintage watches from established brands, thorough research, and a long-term perspective. While this approach requires patience and discipline, it can offer substantial rewards in terms of capital appreciation and the enjoyment of owning historically significant timepieces. By adopting a buy-and-hold strategy, investors can align their investment goals with the long-term potential of vintage watches from these renowned brands.

Timing the market:

Timing the market is a strategy that involves identifying favorable buying opportunities by observing market trends and making purchasing decisions based on perceived undervaluation or market downturns. While timing the market can be challenging and speculative, it can offer potential advantages when investing in vintage watches from these renowned brands. Here, we explore some insights into market timing strategies and their potential benefits.

Buying during market downturns:

Market downturns, when prices of vintage watches may experience a temporary decline, can present attractive opportunities for investors. By carefully monitoring market conditions and recognizing when prices are lower than their historical average, investors can take advantage of these downturns to acquire vintage watches at potentially discounted prices. However, timing market bottoms with precision is difficult, and it's important to conduct thorough research and analysis to ensure the watches are fundamentally sound and have the potential to rebound in value.

Identifying undervalued vintage models:

Vintage watch markets can experience fluctuations in demand and popularity. Certain models or brands may temporarily fall out of favor or be undervalued compared to their intrinsic worth. By staying informed about collector preferences, market trends, and industry developments, investors can identify undervalued vintage models and seize the opportunity to acquire them at favorable prices. This requires extensive research, understanding of the brand's historical significance, and assessing the potential for renewed interest in specific models.

Evaluating historical price trends:

Examining historical price trends and patterns can provide insights into market cycles and help investors make informed decisions. By analyzing past auction records, sales data, and price indices, investors can identify trends in vintage watch pricing and identify potential opportunities. For example, observing upward price trends for specific models or brands may indicate a favorable time to invest before prices escalate further. However, it's important to remember that historical performance is not indicative of future results, and thorough research is necessary to validate any investment decisions.

Seeking expert opinions:

Consulting experts, industry professionals, or vintage watch enthusiasts can provide valuable insights into market timing strategies. Their experience and knowledge can help investors gauge market conditions, identify potential buying opportunities, and understand the factors influencing vintage watch pricing. Engaging with experts can provide a broader perspective and help investors make more informed decisions when it comes to timing the market.

It's essential to approach market timing with caution and understand the inherent risks involved. Predicting short-term market movements is challenging, and attempting to time the market can lead to missed opportunities or potential losses. Investing in vintage watches should primarily be driven by long-term value appreciation, historical significance, and personal enjoyment rather than short-term market fluctuations. A balanced approach that combines a long-term investment horizon, thorough research, and strategic buying opportunities may yield more consistent and favorable results when considering market timing strategies in vintage watch investments.

Risks and considerations in investing in old watch brands:

Market volatility:

Market volatility is an inherent aspect of investing, and vintage watches are not exempt from the impact of market fluctuations. It's crucial for investors to understand the potential risks associated with market volatility and consider them when making investment decisions. Here, we address some key factors that contribute to market volatility and can affect the value of vintage watches.

Changing consumer preferences:

Consumer tastes and preferences can shift over time, influencing the demand for certain vintage watch brands, models, or design aesthetics. What may be highly sought after today may lose popularity in the future. As a result, the value of vintage watches can be impacted by these changing preferences. Investors should stay informed about evolving consumer trends, collector preferences, and market dynamics to anticipate potential shifts in demand.

Economic factors:

Economic conditions, such as recessions, inflation, or geopolitical events, can have a significant impact on the vintage watch market. During economic downturns, consumer spending may decline, leading to decreased demand for luxury items, including vintage watches. Conversely, during periods of economic growth and stability, the demand for luxury watches may increase. Investors should consider the broader economic climate and its potential impact on the vintage watch market when making investment decisions.

Market speculation and hype:

Speculation and hype surrounding certain vintage watches can drive price fluctuations and market volatility. News of rare discoveries, celebrity endorsements, or auctions setting new records can create temporary market excitement and influence prices. However, investors should exercise caution and conduct thorough research to differentiate between genuine investment opportunities and short-lived hype.

Rarity and supply factors:

The availability and supply of vintage watches can significantly impact their value. Limited production numbers, discontinued models, or specific variations with unique features contribute to the rarity and desirability of certain vintage watches. Changes in the supply of these watches, such as new discoveries or significant collections hitting the market, can influence prices and create market volatility.

Counterfeiting and authenticity concerns:

Counterfeit vintage watches pose a significant risk to investors. The presence of counterfeit or replica watches can undermine market confidence and affect the value of genuine vintage watches. It's essential for investors to take measures to verify the authenticity of vintage watches through expert evaluations, research, and consulting reputable sources.

To mitigate the potential risks associated with market volatility, investors should adopt a long-term perspective, focusing on the intrinsic value, historical significance, and authenticity of vintage watches. Diversifying a vintage watch portfolio across different brands, models, and eras can help spread the risk and reduce the impact of individual market fluctuations. Additionally, staying informed about market trends, industry developments, and engaging with knowledgeable experts can provide valuable insights for navigating market volatility.

Investing in vintage watches should be approached with a balanced and informed mindset, considering both the passion for collecting and the potential for long-term appreciation. By understanding and carefully monitoring market volatility, investors can make more informed decisions and navigate the dynamic landscape of vintage watch investments.

Counterfeit and altered watches:

Counterfeit and altered vintage watches pose significant risks to investors, as they can lead to substantial financial losses and damage the reputation of the vintage watch market. It's crucial for investors to be aware of these risks and take necessary precautions to identify and avoid counterfeit or altered watches. Here are some tips to help investors mitigate the risk of encountering fraudulent pieces:

Buy from reputable sources:

Purchase vintage watches from trusted and reputable sources, such as authorized dealers, established auction houses, or reputable vintage watch dealers. These sources are more likely to have stringent authentication processes in place and offer guarantees of authenticity.

Research and educate yourself:

Invest time and effort in researching the specific vintage watch models you're interested in. Familiarize yourself with the authentic features, details, and characteristics of genuine watches from the brand and era you're targeting. Understanding the history, design, and unique elements of each model can help you identify potential red flags.

Examine the watch closely:

Thoroughly inspect the vintage watch for any signs of alteration or counterfeiting. Pay attention to details such as the dial, hands, logo, engravings, and case back. Look for inconsistencies, inaccuracies, or poor craftsmanship that could indicate a counterfeit or altered watch. Compare the watch with reputable reference materials, manufacturer specifications, or authenticated examples to validate its authenticity.

Verify documentation and provenance:

Genuine vintage watches often come with documentation, including certificates of authenticity, original receipts, or service records. Verify the authenticity of these documents and cross-check them with reliable sources if possible. Additionally, consider the watch's provenance and history. Genuine vintage watches may have a documented ownership history or be associated with notable events or individuals.

Seek expert opinion:

When in doubt, consult experts or experienced collectors who specialize in vintage watches. Professional appraisers, horologists, or vintage watch experts can provide valuable insights and authentication services. They have the knowledge and expertise to identify potential counterfeits or alterations that may be difficult for an untrained eye to detect.

Be cautious of deals that seem too good to be true: Exercise caution when encountering deals that offer vintage watches at significantly lower prices than their market value. While occasional opportunities may arise, excessively low prices can be an indication of counterfeit or altered watches. Remember that genuine vintage watches from reputable brands retain value and tend to have a stable or appreciating market price.

Stay informed about counterfeit techniques: Counterfeiters continually evolve their techniques to deceive buyers. Stay updated on the latest counterfeit trends and methods, such as laser etching, cloned serial numbers, or counterfeit documentation. Being aware of these tactics can help you spot potential red flags and make informed purchasing decisions.

By following these guidelines, investors can minimize the risk of purchasing counterfeit or altered vintage watches. It's essential to prioritize authenticity and ensure that the watches in your collection are genuine, as this not only protects your investment but also preserves the integrity and reputation of the vintage watch market.

Expert advice and due diligence:.

Investing in vintage watches requires a diligent and informed approach. To make well-informed investment decisions, it's essential for investors to seek expert advice, conduct thorough research, and exercise due diligence. Here are some key points to consider:

Consult vintage watch experts:

Seek advice from knowledgeable experts in the vintage watch industry. Professional appraisers, experienced collectors, or reputable vintage watch dealers can provide valuable insights, guidance, and recommendations based on their expertise and market knowledge. Their experience can help you navigate the complexities of vintage watch investing and make informed decisions.

Conduct extensive research:

Invest time and effort in conducting thorough research on the vintage watches and brands you're interested in. Explore reputable publications, reference books, online resources, and forums dedicated to vintage watches. Familiarize yourself with the brand's history, notable models, market trends, and pricing dynamics. The more knowledge you acquire, the better equipped you'll be to make informed investment choices.

Stay updated with market trends:

Keep abreast of market trends, industry news, and collector preferences. Monitor auction results, track price fluctuations, and stay informed about the factors that influence the vintage watch market. By staying current, you can identify emerging trends, popular models, and investment opportunities.

Verify authenticity and condition:

Prioritize authenticity and carefully assess the condition of vintage watches before making a purchase. Conduct due diligence to ensure the watch is genuine and in good condition. Verify serial numbers, inspect the watch's components, and assess its overall authenticity. Thoroughly examine the watch for signs of wear, damage, or restoration. Authenticity and condition significantly impact the value and desirability of vintage watches.

Consider the investment horizon:

Determine your investment horizon and align your vintage watch investments accordingly. Vintage watches can be suitable for both short-term and long-term investment strategies. Evaluate your financial goals, risk tolerance, and time horizon to determine whether you're seeking quick returns or aiming for long-term capital appreciation.

Diversify your vintage watch portfolio:

Mitigate risk by diversifying your vintage watch portfolio. Allocate your investments across different brands, models, eras, and price ranges. A well-diversified portfolio can help balance potential risks and capture opportunities from different segments of the vintage watch market.

Keep records and documentation:

Maintain accurate records of your vintage watch collection, including purchase receipts, certificates of authenticity, service records, and any relevant documentation. These records not only serve as proof of ownership but also help establish the authenticity and provenance of your watches, enhancing their value and marketability.

Stay cautious of market fluctuations:

Vintage watch markets can be subject to fluctuations influenced by various factors such as economic conditions, changing consumer preferences, and supply and demand dynamics. Be prepared for market volatility and avoid making impulsive investment decisions based solely on short-term fluctuations.

Take a long-term perspective and consider the intrinsic value and historical performance of the vintage watches you're considering.

By seeking expert advice, conducting thorough research, and exercising due diligence, investors can make informed decisions and minimize risks when investing in vintage watches. Remember that vintage watch investing requires a combination of passion, knowledge, and careful consideration of the market dynamics to achieve successful outcomes.

Part 4: Market Trends and Future Outlook

The vintage watch market is a fascinating realm where tastes, preferences, and market dynamics continuously evolve. Understanding the trends that drive the market can be instrumental in making informed investment decisions and capitalizing on emerging opportunities. By studying the market trends, you can gain valuable insights into the shifting landscape of vintage watches.

Looking to the future, we explore the potential developments and innovations that may shape the vintage watch industry. We analyze emerging markets, advancements in technology, and changing consumer behavior to paint a picture of what the future may hold. By anticipating these developments, you can position yourself strategically and capitalize on future opportunities.

We consider the importance of sustainability and ethical considerations in the vintage watch market. As societal values evolve, so does the demand for responsible practices and sustainable approaches to watch collecting and investing. We delve into the implications of sustainability in the vintage watch market and highlight the opportunities it presents for conscientious collectors and investors.

Evolving market trends in vintage watch collecting:

Shifting collector preferences:

In the ever-evolving world of vintage watch collecting, the preferences and desires of collectors shape the market trends and future outlook. As time progresses, collector tastes undergo transformations, influenced by a myriad of factors ranging from cultural shifts to emerging fashion trends. This section offers a deep dive into the fascinating realm of shifting collector preferences and the profound impact they have on the vintage watch market.

Vintage watch collecting is not static but rather a dynamic landscape that experiences waves of changing trends and evolving styles. What was highly sought after a decade ago may no longer captivate collectors' attention today. As we explore this captivating topic, we delve into the current state of vintage watch collecting, unearthing the emerging trends that are reshaping the market.

Styles and designs that were once overlooked or underappreciated can experience a renaissance, fuelled by nostalgia, a renewed appreciation for their uniqueness, or a reevaluation of their artistic and aesthetic value. The market has witnessed a resurgence of interest in vintage watches from specific eras, such as the elegant and minimalist designs of the mid-20th century or the bold and audacious styles of the 1980s. By examining these shifts in preferences, we enable collectors and investors to anticipate emerging opportunities and adapt their strategies accordingly.

We venture into the realm of brand preferences and the shifting dynamics of brand desirability in the vintage watch market. Some brands have achieved legendary status, with their vintage models commanding premium prices and generating fervent enthusiasm among collectors. However, the landscape is not static, and the fortunes of brands can change over time. Brand popularity can be influenced by various factors, including cultural references, celebrity endorsements, or reissues of iconic models. By understanding these nuances, collectors and investors can make well-informed decisions when acquiring vintage watches.

We explore the demand for specific models within a brand's lineup. Some vintage watch models have become highly sought after due to their scarcity, historical significance, or unique design features, while others may experience a decline in demand as collector tastes shift towards different styles or eras. By discerning these shifts, collectors and investors gain valuable insights into market dynamics, enabling them to strategically navigate the vintage watch market.

Understanding the ever-changing landscape of collector preferences offers a window into the trends that drive the vintage watch industry. With each passing generation, new collectors emerge, bringing fresh perspectives and evolving tastes. This, coupled with broader societal shifts, ensures that the vintage watch market remains in a state of constant flux. By staying attuned to shifting collector preferences, emerging trends, and popular styles, collectors and investors can adapt their strategies to align with the evolving market landscape.

Embark on a captivating journey as we explore the mesmerizing world of shifting collector preferences, uncovering emerging trends, and gaining a deeper understanding of the dynamic nature of vintage watch collecting. Discover the styles, brands, and models that capture the imagination of collectors, and gain valuable insights that will inform your decision-making process. The ever-changing vintage watch market awaits, brimming with possibilities for those with a keen eye and a passion for timeless timepieces.

Influence of social media and online communities:

In the digital age, social media has become an influential force that shapes various aspects of our lives, including the world of vintage watch collecting. The rise of social media platforms and online communities has revolutionized the way collectors connect, share their passion, and stay informed about the latest trends. This section delves into the profound impact of social media and online communities on the vintage watch market, shedding light on how these platforms have transformed the industry.

Social media platforms such as Instagram, Facebook, and YouTube have become virtual gathering places for vintage watch enthusiasts. They provide a platform for collectors to showcase their prized timepieces, share their knowledge and experiences, and engage in vibrant discussions with like-minded individuals from around the world. The power of social media lies in its ability to connect collectors, creating a global network where ideas, opinions, and discoveries can be shared instantaneously.

One of the key ways social media has influenced the vintage watch market is through the dissemination of information and trends. Collectors now have access to an abundance of content, including detailed watch reviews, historical insights, and market analysis, all readily available at their fingertips. This wealth of information empowers collectors to make informed decisions, stay up to date with the latest market trends, and discover hidden gems within the vintage watch landscape.

Social media has played a significant role in shaping and amplifying trends within the vintage watch community. Influencers, bloggers, and industry experts utilize these platforms to showcase their personal collections, highlight notable acquisitions, and provide recommendations to their followers. Their opinions and preferences can quickly gain traction, leading to a surge in demand for specific brands, models, or styles. The viral nature of social media allows trends to spread rapidly, creating a ripple effect throughout the vintage watch market.

Online communities dedicated to vintage watches have also emerged as valuable resources for collectors. Forums, discussion boards, and specialized websites bring together individuals who share a passion for vintage timepieces. These communities foster an environment of knowledge-sharing, where enthusiasts can seek advice, exchange information, and engage in lively conversations. Online marketplaces dedicated to vintage watches have also gained popularity, providing a convenient platform for collectors to buy and sell timepieces, expanding the reach and accessibility of the vintage watch market.

It is important to note that the influence of social media and online communities also brings certain challenges. The vast amount of information available online can be overwhelming, and collectors need to exercise caution and discernment when evaluating opinions and recommendations. Additionally, the viral nature of trends on social media can sometimes create inflated prices or excessive demand for certain models, potentially impacting the market dynamics.

The advent of social media and online communities has undeniably brought about a democratization of knowledge and access to the vintage watch market. Collectors now have unprecedented opportunities to connect, learn, and participate in the vibrant vintage watch community. The influence of social media platforms and online communities is reshaping the market, creating new opportunities for collectors to discover rare timepieces, stay informed about market trends, and connect with fellow enthusiasts.

As we explore the influence of social media and online communities on the vintage watch market, we uncover the transformative power of these platforms. From shaping trends and driving demand to providing a global network of like-minded individuals, social media and online communities have become integral components of the vintage watch collecting experience. Join us as we delve into the fascinating intersection of technology, community, and vintage watches, and gain insights into how these digital platforms are shaping the future of the market.

Market dynamics and competition:

The vintage watch market is a dynamic and competitive arena, shaped by various players vying for the attention of collectors and investors. This section delves into the market dynamics and competition that characterize the vintage watch industry, shedding light on the key players and their roles in driving the market forward.

Auction houses play a significant role in the vintage watch market, serving as platforms where rare and exceptional timepieces are bought and sold. Renowned auction houses such as Sotheby's, Christie's, and Phillips have dedicated watch departments that curate and present high-profile watch auctions, attracting collectors, enthusiasts, and investors from around the globe. These auctions offer a unique opportunity to acquire exceptional vintage watches with provenance, historical significance, and exceptional craftsmanship. The competitive bidding environment created by auction houses often leads to record-breaking sales and sets benchmarks for market values.

In addition to auction houses, authorized dealers and independent watch dealers play a crucial role in the vintage watch market. Authorized dealers represent brands directly and provide collectors with access to new and pre-owned timepieces. They offer a level of trust, authenticity, and after-sales service that collectors value. Independent watch dealers, on the other hand, specialize in sourcing, curating, and selling vintage watches from various brands. They often have extensive networks and expertise in the vintage watch market, providing collectors with a wide range of options and insights.

The advent of online platforms has transformed the vintage watch market, creating new avenues for buying, selling, and connecting. Online marketplaces, such as Chrono24, WatchBox, and Bob's Watches, have gained popularity and offer a vast selection of vintage watches from different brands, eras, and price points. These platforms provide collectors with convenience, accessibility, and a global reach, allowing them to browse and purchase watches from the comfort of their homes. Online forums and communities also play a role in facilitating transactions and sharing knowledge within the vintage watch community.

Competition within the vintage watch market is fierce, with dealers and platforms constantly seeking to attract collectors and differentiate themselves. They employ various strategies to stand out, including offering exclusive inventory, providing expert knowledge and authentication services, and ensuring exceptional customer service. The competitive landscape drives innovation and the continuous improvement of offerings, benefitting collectors who have a wider range of options and resources at their disposal.

Market dynamics within the vintage watch industry are also influenced by factors such as supply and demand dynamics, economic conditions, and shifting consumer preferences. The rarity, condition, and historical significance of vintage watches significantly impact their value and desirability. As certain brands, models, or styles gain popularity, competition among collectors and investors intensifies, leading to potential price increases. Conversely, market trends and shifts in demand can also affect the market dynamics, leading to fluctuations in prices and the emergence of new investment opportunities.

Understanding the competitive landscape and market dynamics is essential for collectors and investors navigating the vintage watch market. It allows them to make informed decisions, identify reliable sources for acquiring watches, and stay ahead of emerging trends. By analyzing the presence of auction houses, dealers, and online platforms, collectors gain a comprehensive view of the ecosystem in which vintage watches are bought and sold.

As we analyze the market dynamics and competition within the vintage watch industry, we gain insights into the key players, their roles, and the factors that shape the market. By understanding the interplay between auction houses, dealers, and online platforms, collectors and investors can navigate the vintage watch market with confidence and make informed decisions. Join us as we delve into the competitive landscape and explore the dynamics that drive this fascinating industry forward.

The impact of technology and innovation on vintage watch brands:

Technological advancements in the watch industry:

In an era driven by technological innovation, the watch industry has also witnessed significant advancements that have shaped the way we perceive and appreciate vintage watches. This section explores the influence of modern technology, particularly the rise of smartwatches and digital timekeeping, on the vintage watch market.

Smartwatches have emerged as a distinct category within the watch industry, integrating advanced technology with traditional timekeeping. These intelligent timepieces offer a range of features beyond mere timekeeping, including fitness tracking, smartphone notifications, and various apps. The advent of smartwatches has introduced a new dimension to the wristwatch landscape, appealing to tech-savvy consumers and those seeking a blend of functionality and style.

The rise of smartwatches has undoubtedly impacted the perception and appreciation of vintage watches. Some argue that smartwatches have disrupted the market, diverting attention and demand away from traditional mechanical watches. However, others maintain that the two categories cater to different consumer preferences and can coexist harmoniously. In fact, the presence of smartwatches has prompted a renewed appreciation for the craftsmanship, heritage, and timeless appeal of vintage watches. Many collectors and enthusiasts view vintage watches as a symbol of tradition, artistry, and enduring value, contrasting with the ephemeral nature of technology-driven gadgets.

Digital timekeeping, beyond smartwatches, has also influenced the perception and appreciation of vintage watches. The prevalence of digital clocks on various electronic devices, such as smartphones and computers, has made traditional mechanical timepieces stand out even more. Vintage watches offer a distinct experience, showcasing the intricate mechanical movements and the artistry involved in their construction. The analog display of time, the ticking of the hands, and the precision of mechanical components create a unique connection with the wearer that cannot be replicated by digital timekeeping.

It is important to note that while modern technology has brought advancements to the watch industry, vintage watches maintain their allure and appeal. The craftsmanship, design, and historical significance of vintage timepieces continue to captivate collectors and enthusiasts. Vintage watches represent a tangible connection to the past, carrying with them stories, legacies, and the embodiment of the watchmaking artistry of a bygone era.

The influence of modern technology in the form of smartwatches and digital timekeeping has both direct and indirect effects on the vintage watch market. The presence of smartwatches has expanded the options available to consumers, catering to different tastes and preferences. At the same time, it has reminded enthusiasts of the timeless charm and intrinsic value of vintage watches. The enduring appeal of vintage watches lies in their ability to transcend technology and provide a sense of tradition, craftsmanship, and emotional connection.

As we examine the influence of modern technology on the perception and appreciation of vintage watches, we gain a deeper understanding of the evolving landscape of the watch industry. The coexistence of smartwatches and vintage timepieces offers a diverse range of choices for consumers, each with its own distinct characteristics and appeal. By embracing technological advancements while cherishing the heritage and craftsmanship of vintage watches, collectors and enthusiasts can navigate the ever-changing market and find a timepiece that resonates with their individual preferences.

Collecting vintage watches in the digital age:

In the digital age, the world of vintage watch collecting has undergone a significant transformation. The advent of digital platforms, online marketplaces, and virtual experiences has revolutionized the way collectors explore, acquire, and engage with vintage watches. This section delves into how these digital advancements have impacted the accessibility and visibility of vintage watches, opening up new possibilities for collectors worldwide.

Digital platforms have emerged as a vital tool for collectors, providing a wealth of information, resources, and connections within the vintage watch community. Websites, forums, and social media platforms dedicated to horology have become gathering places for enthusiasts to share their passion, exchange knowledge, and discover rare timepieces. These digital platforms enable collectors to access a vast array of information about vintage watches, including historical details, specifications, pricing trends, and expert opinions. The ability to connect with like-minded individuals from around the globe fosters a sense of community and creates opportunities for collaboration and learning.

Online marketplaces have revolutionized the buying and selling of vintage watches. These platforms provide a convenient and accessible avenue for collectors to acquire timepieces from trusted sellers and dealers worldwide. The vast inventory available on online marketplaces allows collectors to explore a diverse range of vintage watches, spanning different brands, models, and price points. The ability to browse through extensive catalogs, view detailed photographs, and read comprehensive descriptions provides collectors with a level of transparency and convenience that was previously unimaginable. Online marketplaces also facilitate secure transactions, with trusted payment systems and buyer protection policies, giving collectors confidence in their purchasing decisions.

Virtual experiences have further enhanced the accessibility and visibility of vintage watches. Online exhibitions, virtual tours, and digital showcases offer immersive and interactive experiences for collectors to explore rare and exceptional timepieces. Through high-resolution imagery, detailed descriptions, and multimedia presentations, virtual experiences bring the beauty and craftsmanship of vintage watches directly to enthusiasts' screens. These digital platforms also enable collectors to participate in live auctions and bidding, expanding their access to highly sought-after timepieces that may be located in different parts of the world. The ability to engage with vintage watches in a virtual environment transcends geographical boundaries and time constraints, enriching the collecting experience.

The impact of digital platforms, online marketplaces, and virtual experiences extends beyond accessibility. These digital advancements have also increased the visibility of vintage watches, creating a global marketplace and fostering a broader appreciation for horological treasures. Collectors can now showcase their own vintage watch collections to a wider audience through social media platforms, blogs, and dedicated websites. The ability to share photographs, stories, and insights about their timepieces not only allows collectors to connect with fellow enthusiasts but also promotes the appreciation and understanding of vintage watches among a broader community.

It is important to navigate the digital landscape with caution. As the popularity of vintage watches grows, so does the risk of encountering counterfeit or misrepresented timepieces. Collectors must exercise due diligence, relying on reputable sellers, verifying the authenticity of watches, and seeking expert advice when needed. Additionally, while digital platforms offer convenience and accessibility, the tactile experience of holding and examining a vintage watch in person remains unparalleled. Thus, collectors should strive to strike a balance between the digital realm and physical interactions with timepieces.

As the world becomes increasingly interconnected, collecting vintage watches in the digital age offers an exciting and dynamic landscape for enthusiasts. The accessibility, information, and global reach provided by digital platforms, online marketplaces, and virtual experiences have transformed the collecting experience, allowing collectors to explore a vast universe of vintage watches from the comfort of their own screens. By embracing these digital advancements while maintaining a discerning eye, collectors can expand their horizons, make informed decisions, and continue to foster their passion for vintage watches.

Future possibilities:

The world of vintage watch collecting is not immune to technological advancements, and as we look to the future, there are exciting possibilities that may revolutionize the way collectors engage with and appreciate vintage timepieces. This section explores some potential developments that could shape the future of vintage watch collecting, offering a glimpse into the possibilities that lie ahead.

One area of great interest is the application of blockchain technology in authenticating vintage watches. Blockchain, the decentralized and transparent digital ledger, has gained prominence in various industries, and its potential in the luxury market, including vintage watches, is intriguing. By leveraging blockchain technology, it may be possible to create immutable and tamper-proof records of a watch's provenance, ownership history, and authenticity. This would provide collectors with an unprecedented level of confidence and trust in the vintage watch market, eliminating concerns about counterfeit or altered timepieces. Blockchain authentication could create a secure and verifiable system that ensures the integrity of vintage watches and enhances their value in the eyes of collectors.

Augmented reality (AR) experiences hold immense potential in enriching the collecting journey for vintage watch enthusiasts. Imagine being able to virtually try on rare and coveted timepieces, exploring their intricate details, and experiencing their mechanisms in a highly immersive digital environment. Augmented reality could offer collectors the opportunity to interact with virtual versions of vintage watches, allowing them to visualize how the timepiece would look on their wrist or examine its intricate components with unparalleled detail. Such experiences would enhance the accessibility and engagement with vintage watches, transcending the limitations of physical proximity and creating a truly captivating and interactive collecting experience.

Another intriguing possibility is the digitization of ownership records and historical documentation. In the digital age, the preservation and accessibility of provenance information play a crucial role in determining the value and authenticity of vintage watches. Digitized ownership records could ensure that important historical documentation, including original sales receipts, service records, and previous ownership details, are securely stored and easily accessible. This digitization would not only provide collectors with a comprehensive and organized archive but also facilitate research and verification processes. Collectors could access a watch's complete history at their fingertips, contributing to a more transparent and informed marketplace.

The integration of artificial intelligence (AI) and machine learning algorithms could revolutionize the way vintage watches are valued and appraised. AI-powered systems could analyze vast amounts of historical data, including auction records, sales trends, and market fluctuations, to provide collectors with real-time insights into the value and potential growth prospects of vintage watches. These intelligent systems could help collectors make more informed investment decisions, identify emerging trends, and navigate the complexities of the vintage watch market with greater precision.

While these future possibilities are exciting, it is important to remember that technological advancements should be approached with caution and careful consideration. Preserving the authenticity, heritage, and craftsmanship of vintage watches should remain paramount, even as new technologies are embraced. The tactile experience of handling a vintage watch, appreciating its intricate details, and connecting with its history should not be overshadowed by digital innovations but rather enhanced by them.

As we gaze into the future, it is clear that technological advancements hold immense potential to shape the world of vintage watch collecting. Blockchain authentication, augmented reality experiences, digitized ownership records, and AI-powered insights are just a few examples of how technology could transform the collecting landscape. By embracing these innovations while upholding the core values of vintage watch collecting, enthusiasts can look forward to an exciting and dynamic future where the past and the present coexist in harmony.

Regional variations and emerging markets in vintage watch collecting:

Global market dynamics:

Vintage watch collecting is a global phenomenon, with enthusiasts and collectors spanning across continents and cultures. While the allure of vintage watches transcends borders, there are distinct regional variations in collecting preferences, market dynamics, and the demand for specific brands and models. Understanding these regional nuances is essential for collectors and investors seeking to navigate the global vintage watch market successfully.

Cultural preferences play a significant role in shaping the demand for vintage watches in different regions. For example, in Europe, where many iconic watch brands originated, there is a deep appreciation for traditional craftsmanship, heritage, and timeless elegance. Brands like Rolex, Patek Philippe, and Omega are highly sought after in this region, as they embody the essence of classic watchmaking.

In North America, there is a diverse and eclectic mix of collecting preferences. While established luxury brands like Rolex and Omega enjoy popularity, there is also a growing interest in vintage watches from independent or niche brands that offer unique designs, limited editions, or avant-garde aesthetics. Collectors in North America often value individuality and seek out timepieces that stand out from the crowd.

In Asia, particularly in countries like China, Japan, and Hong Kong, there is a strong appetite for luxury goods, including vintage watches. Asian collectors are known for their discerning taste and a preference for brands with strong historical significance, such as Rolex and Patek Philippe. Additionally, the rise of the Asian market has also led to increased demand for vintage watches from regional brands like Seiko and Citizen, which have gained recognition for their precision and craftsmanship.

Historical significance also plays a crucial role in regional variations. Watches associated with significant historical events or cultural icons hold particular appeal in their respective regions. For example, timepieces linked to exploration and adventure, such as Rolex watches worn by mountaineers or Omega Speedmasters worn by astronauts, are highly valued in markets with a strong interest in exploration and space exploration history.

Economic factors also influence the vintage watch market on a global scale. Economic growth, disposable income levels, and currency fluctuations can impact both the demand and pricing of vintage watches. In regions experiencing rapid economic growth, there is often a rise in the number of affluent collectors seeking to invest in luxury items, including vintage watches. This increased demand can drive up prices for certain brands and models. On the other hand, economic downturns or currency devaluations may present buying opportunities for collectors looking to acquire vintage watches at more favorable prices.

It is important to note that while there are regional variations in vintage watch collecting, the global market is highly interconnected. Online platforms, international auctions, and the ease of global communication have brought collectors from different regions together, creating a truly global marketplace. Collectors can now easily access and acquire vintage watches from around the world, allowing for a diverse and dynamic collecting experience.

By understanding the regional variations in vintage watch collecting, collectors and investors can gain valuable insights into market trends, demand patterns, and pricing dynamics. This knowledge enables them to make informed decisions, identify opportunities, and build a well-rounded and diverse vintage watch collection that appeals to a global audience.

As the vintage watch market continues to evolve, it is essential to stay attuned to the cultural, historical, and economic factors shaping regional preferences. Embracing the global nature of vintage watch collecting allows enthusiasts to appreciate the rich diversity of timepieces, connect with collectors from different backgrounds, and participate in a vibrant and ever-changing market.

Emerging markets and growing interest:

The vintage watch market has experienced a significant shift in recent years, with the emergence of new markets and a growing interest in vintage watches from regions outside of the traditional strongholds. Countries in Asia, the Middle East, and Latin America have witnessed a surge in enthusiasm for vintage watches, reshaping the dynamics of the overall market and influencing global collecting trends.

Asia, in particular, has emerged as a powerhouse in the vintage watch market. Countries like China, Japan, Hong Kong, and Singapore have experienced rapid economic growth, resulting in an expanding middle class with an increased purchasing power. This economic growth has fueled a growing interest in luxury goods, including vintage watches. Asian collectors are drawn to the craftsmanship, heritage, and prestige associated with vintage watches, making brands like Rolex, Patek Philippe, and Omega highly sought after in the region. The demand from Asian collectors has not only influenced pricing but has also led to the establishment of dedicated vintage watch boutiques, auctions, and collector communities catering to their specific preferences.

The Middle East is another region that has seen a surge in interest in vintage watches. Countries like the United Arab Emirates, Qatar, and Saudi Arabia have experienced rapid development and have become luxury hubs, attracting high-net-worth individuals with a penchant for exclusive timepieces. The Middle Eastern market has a particular affinity for prestigious brands like Rolex, Audemars Piguet, and Patek Philippe, appreciating their timeless designs, intricate complications, and investment value. This growing interest has resulted in dedicated vintage watch events, exhibitions, and boutiques in the region, further fueling the demand for vintage watches.

Latin America is also witnessing a rise in the appreciation for vintage watches. Countries like Brazil, Mexico, and Argentina have seen a growing collector base that values the craftsmanship and heritage associated with vintage timepieces. Vintage watch enthusiasts in Latin America often seek out iconic brands like Rolex, Omega, and Cartier, recognizing their historical significance and enduring appeal. As the interest in vintage watches continues to grow, Latin America has seen the establishment of specialized vintage watch dealers, auctions, and collector communities, creating a vibrant and thriving market in the region.

The emergence of these new markets and the increased interest in vintage watches from Asia, the Middle East, and Latin America have had a significant impact on the overall market. The influx of new collectors has expanded the collector base, creating a greater demand for vintage watches and driving up prices for certain brands and models. The interest from these regions has also influenced market trends and preferences, with a focus on brands known for their craftsmanship, heritage, and investment value.

The global nature of the vintage watch market has been further enhanced by online platforms and international auctions, allowing collectors from different regions to access a wide range of vintage watches and participate in the market. This interconnectedness has resulted in increased visibility and accessibility for vintage watches from these emerging markets, attracting collectors and investors from around the world.

As these emerging markets continue to grow and develop, their impact on the vintage watch market is expected to deepen. The evolving preferences and buying behaviors of collectors from Asia, the Middle East, and Latin America will shape market trends, influence pricing dynamics, and contribute to the overall vibrancy of the vintage watch market.

The emergence of new markets and the growing interest in vintage watches from regions such as Asia, the Middle East, and Latin America have brought new dynamics and opportunities to the vintage watch market. The passion for vintage watches is transcending borders, as collectors from around the world appreciate the craftsmanship, heritage, and timeless appeal of these timepieces. As the global vintage watch community continues to expand, it opens up exciting possibilities for collectors, investors, and enthusiasts alike.

Future outlook and potential challenges:

Sustainability and ethical considerations:

In recent years, there has been a notable shift in consumer attitudes towards sustainability and ethical practices in various industries, including the watch industry. This shift is driven by a growing awareness of environmental issues, social responsibility, and the desire to make conscious purchasing decisions. As a result, sustainability and ethical considerations have become important factors influencing consumer preferences and shaping market trends, including the vintage watch market.

The watch industry, like many other luxury sectors, has recognized the need to embrace sustainability and ethical practices. There is an increasing focus on reducing the environmental impact of manufacturing processes, ensuring responsible sourcing of materials, and promoting fair labor practices. Sustainable initiatives include using recycled or responsibly sourced precious metals, implementing energy-efficient production methods, and supporting social and community development programs.

These sustainability and ethical practices extend to the vintage watch market as well. Vintage watches inherently promote sustainability by providing a way to reuse and appreciate existing timepieces, reducing the demand for new production. Collecting vintage watches aligns with the principles of sustainability and recycling, as it allows for the preservation and enjoyment of timepieces from the past.

There is a growing demand for vintage watches that have been restored or serviced using sustainable and eco-friendly methods. Collectors and buyers are increasingly seeking out watchmakers and restoration experts who prioritize environmentally friendly practices, such as using non-toxic cleaning agents, minimizing waste, and employing energy-efficient techniques. This emphasis on sustainability in the restoration process adds an additional layer of value to vintage watches.

Ethical considerations also play a significant role in the vintage watch market. With increasing awareness of labor practices and the responsible sourcing of materials, collectors are placing importance on the authenticity and ethical origins of vintage watches. Ensuring that vintage watches have not been associated with unethical practices, such as conflict minerals or unauthorized modifications, has become a priority for both collectors and industry stakeholders.

The emphasis on sustainability and ethical practices in the watch industry has the potential to shape the vintage watch market in several ways. Firstly, it may influence collector preferences, with individuals seeking out vintage watches from brands known for their commitment to sustainability and ethical conduct. Brands that align with these values may experience increased desirability and demand in the vintage watch market.

The adoption of sustainable practices by watch manufacturers and restoration experts may result in improved transparency and documentation, providing collectors with confidence in the authenticity and ethical origins of vintage watches. This transparency can contribute to the growth and credibility of the vintage watch market, fostering trust among collectors and investors.

The integration of sustainability and ethical considerations may drive innovation in the vintage watch market. For example, advancements in eco-friendly restoration techniques, the use of alternative materials, or the adoption of sustainable packaging solutions can create new opportunities for collectors and add value to vintage watches.

Sustainability and ethical considerations have become integral aspects of the watch industry, including the vintage watch market. The growing importance of these principles reflects the changing consumer landscape and the desire for conscious consumption. As sustainability and ethical practices continue to gain traction, they will likely shape the preferences, values, and market dynamics of vintage watch collectors, promoting a more responsible and sustainable approach to preserving and appreciating timepieces from the past.

Regulatory changes and compliance:

The vintage watch market operates within a broader regulatory landscape that governs the sale and distribution of timepieces. Over time, regulatory changes and compliance requirements can present challenges for sellers, dealers, collectors, and investors in the vintage watch market. It is important to stay informed about these developments to ensure compliance and navigate any potential hurdles.

One area of concern is the regulations surrounding the trade of rare or antique materials used in vintage watches, such as certain types of exotic animal leathers, ivory, or precious metals. As conservation efforts and animal welfare concerns gain prominence, there may be restrictions or bans on the use and trade of certain materials. These regulations can impact the availability and value of vintage watches that incorporate such materials. Collectors and sellers must be aware of these regulations to avoid legal complications and ethical dilemmas.

There may be evolving regulations related to the authentication and certification of vintage watches. As counterfeiting practices become more sophisticated, governments and industry organizations may introduce stricter measures to combat the sale of counterfeit or altered timepieces. Compliance with authentication processes, certification requirements, and transparency in disclosing the condition and history of vintage watches can become more crucial.

Changes in tax regulations and import/export laws can affect the cross-border trade of vintage watches. Tariffs, duties, and customs regulations may vary between countries, leading to potential challenges in shipping, selling, or acquiring vintage watches internationally. It is essential for collectors and sellers to understand these regulations and seek professional advice to ensure compliance and navigate the complexities of international trade.

Data protection and privacy regulations are also important considerations in the digital age. Online platforms and marketplaces that facilitate the sale of vintage watches must adhere to data privacy laws to protect the personal information of buyers and sellers. Compliance with these regulations is essential for maintaining trust and ensuring secure transactions in the online vintage watch market.

As regulatory changes occur, industry associations and organizations play a crucial role in providing guidance and resources to navigate compliance requirements. These organizations often collaborate with governments and regulatory bodies to establish industry standards, certification processes, and best practices for the vintage watch market.

While regulatory changes and compliance requirements may present challenges, they are ultimately aimed at protecting consumers, preserving the integrity of the market, and addressing ethical concerns. It is important for collectors, sellers, and investors in the vintage watch market to stay informed, adapt to evolving regulations, and seek professional advice when needed.

Regulatory changes and compliance requirements can impact the sale and distribution of vintage watches. From restrictions on rare materials to authentication processes, tax regulations, and data protection, compliance with evolving regulations is essential. Staying informed, seeking expert advice, and adhering to industry standards will help collectors, sellers, and investors navigate potential challenges and ensure a transparent and compliant vintage watch market.

Predictions and speculations:

The vintage watch market has witnessed significant growth and evolution over the years, driven by a combination of historical appreciation, collector demand, and evolving market dynamics. Looking ahead, several trends and factors may shape the future of the vintage watch market, presenting both opportunities and challenges for collectors and investors.

The demand for vintage watches is expected to continue its upward trajectory. As the appreciation for craftsmanship, heritage, and uniqueness grows, more individuals are likely to be drawn to the charm and character of vintage timepieces. This increased demand, coupled with limited supply, can contribute to the appreciation of vintage watch values, particularly for rare and sought-after models.

The influence of emerging markets, such as Asia, the Middle East, and Latin America, is expected to play a significant role in shaping the vintage watch market's future. These regions have seen a growing interest in luxury goods, including vintage watches, driven by factors such as rising disposable incomes, increasing brand awareness, and a desire for tangible assets with enduring value. As collectors and investors from these markets enter the vintage watch scene, it can lead to new trends, market dynamics, and potential price growth for certain brands and models.

Technological advancements are also likely to impact the vintage watch market. While vintage watches embody traditional craftsmanship and mechanical movements, modern technologies such as blockchain authentication, augmented reality experiences, and digitized ownership records have the potential to enhance transparency, traceability, and the overall collector experience. These innovations can provide additional layers of confidence and trust, especially when it comes to verifying authenticity, ownership history, and provenance.

Alongside these positive developments, challenges and considerations must be acknowledged. One such challenge is the preservation of vintage watch authenticity and originality in a market that faces increasing instances of counterfeiting and alterations. The ability to distinguish genuine vintage watches from counterfeit or modified pieces will remain crucial, and advancements in authentication techniques and expertise will play a pivotal role in maintaining the integrity of the market.

The vintage watch market is not immune to economic fluctuations and broader market trends. Economic conditions, consumer sentiment, and geopolitical factors can influence buyer behavior, investment strategies, and pricing dynamics. Staying informed about global economic trends and their potential impact on the vintage watch market will be essential for collectors and investors seeking to make informed decisions.

In terms of investment opportunities, the vintage watch market offers a diverse range of options. While certain iconic brands like Rolex, Omega, Patek Philippe, and Audemars Piguet have historically been favored by collectors, there may also be potential in exploring niche or regional brands that offer unique designs, craftsmanship, or historical significance. Diversifying a vintage watch investment portfolio across different brands, models, and eras can help mitigate risks and maximize potential returns.

As with any investment, thorough research, due diligence, and expert advice are crucial. Staying informed about market trends, industry developments, and collector preferences can provide valuable insights into potential investment opportunities. Engaging with reputable sources, attending auctions, joining collector communities, and leveraging the expertise of industry professionals can help navigate the complexities of the vintage watch market and make informed investment decisions.

The future outlook of the vintage watch market holds both opportunities and challenges. The growing demand, emerging markets, technological advancements, and investment potential indicate a positive trajectory for vintage watches. However, preserving authenticity, understanding market dynamics, and being aware of economic factors are vital considerations. By staying informed, conducting thorough research, and seeking expert advice, collectors and investors can position themselves to capitalize on the evolving trends and potential investment opportunities that the vintage watch market offers.

Conclusion

Throughout the book, we have delved into the allure and growth of vintage watch collecting, highlighting its historical significance, design aesthetics, and the contributions of established luxury brands like Rolex, Omega, Patek Philippe, and Audemars Piguet. We have also examined the appeal of regional or niche brands, rarity and collectibility, and the impact of historical context, provenance, and design on the desirability and market value of vintage watches.

The book has offered valuable insights into the evolving preferences and trends of vintage watch collectors, helping readers understand the shifting landscape of brand popularity, model preferences, and design eras. We have explored different collecting strategies, preservation and restoration considerations, and provided expert tips for building a well-curated vintage watch collection. Additionally, we have discussed the investment aspects of vintage watches, including market trends, pricing dynamics, and factors to consider when investing in these timeless timepieces.

Throughout the book, we have emphasized the importance of authenticity verification, providing readers with essential tips and methods to ensure the genuineness of vintage watches. We have also highlighted the role of market volatility, counterfeit watches, and the need for due diligence when making investment decisions. By addressing these critical aspects, readers are equipped with the knowledge and tools to navigate the vintage watch market confidently.

Looking towards the future, we have explored market trends and the impact of technological advancements, such as the influence of social media, online communities, and digital platforms on vintage watch collecting. We have also discussed emerging markets, sustainability considerations, regulatory changes, and the potential of technological innovations to shape the future of the vintage watch market.

In conclusion, this book serves as a comprehensive guide for both vintage watch enthusiasts and investors. It offers a deep understanding of the historical significance, craftsmanship, and design aesthetics of vintage watches. Moreover, it provides valuable insights into market dynamics, collector preferences, and investment considerations, empowering readers to make informed decisions and navigate the ever-evolving landscape of vintage watch collecting.

Whether you are a passionate collector seeking to expand your knowledge or an investor looking to explore the potential of vintage watches as a lucrative asset, this book serves as an indispensable resource. By leveraging the expertise shared within these pages, you are well-equipped to embark on your own journey into the captivating world of vintage watches, appreciate their timeless beauty, and make informed decisions that align with your passion and investment goals.

So, take a step back in time, immerse yourself in the rich history of old watch brands, and embrace the excitement of collecting and investing in these cherished timepieces. The world of vintage watches awaits, ready to captivate you with its craftsmanship, design, and enduring value.